"The Realities of [...] insights into the creation p[...] all possibilities and addresses all perspectives. If you don't get it in one chapter, you'll get it in another!"
—DeeWallace, actor, author, and healer

"If you are ready to change your life—and experience lasting change—then this book is for you! In *The Realities of Creation*, you will have the opportunity to explore some of life's greatest questions, especially, "How do I create my dream life?" Take the time to carefully read through the chapters to delve into your life's purpose, develop emotional mastery, shift your perspective, discover the power of your heart—and so much more!"
—Ursula Mentjes, author of *Selling with Intention, Selling with Synchronicity* and *One Great Goal*

"The wisdom of the authors in *The Realities of Creation* act as ancient yet contemporary temple goddesses, here to shepherd humanity into a higher, yet more grounded way to live the dream of heaven on Earth."
—Kelly Sullivan Walden, author of *It's All in Your Dreams* and *I Had the Strangest Dream*

THE
REALITIES
of
CREATION

Dear Iré ♥
You are an
amazing reflection of spirit
a lovely aspect of
here on earth. As you
model that everyone
the world - a) everyone
is blessed & b) all
of reality changes!
Love,
Jan

THE
REALITIES
of
CREATION

Moving Beyond the Limitations of Our Beliefs

JEAN ADRIENNE
Leslie Amerson • Julia Griffin
Laurie Huston • Kathleen O'Keefe Kanavos
Linda Minnick • Maureen St. Germain
Suzanne Strisower • Lynn Waldrop

RAINBOW RIDGE
BOOKS

Cover and interior design by Frame25 Productions
Cover photo © Shutterstock.com

Published by:
Rainbow Ridge Books, LLC
140 Rainbow Ridge Road
Faber, Virginia 22938
434-361-1723

If you are unable to order this book from your local
bookseller, you may order directly from the distributor.

Square One Publishers, Inc.
115 Herricks Road
Garden City Park, NY 11040
Phone: (516) 535-2010
Fax: (516) 535-2014
Toll-free: 877-900-BOOK

Library of Congress Cataloging-in-Publication Data applied for.

ISBN 978-1-937907-41-9

10 9 8 7 6 5 4 3 2 1

Printed on acid-free recycled paper in Canada

TABLE OF CONTENTS

INTRODUCTION

Have you ever played with imagining what you would wish for if you found Aladdin's lamp and the Genie inside? I used to spend *hours* pondering what my three wishes would be and how they might impact my life.

What I have come to realize is that doing this and actually *believing* you can have your wishes come true is a major step forward in creating it to happen! If you can conceive something, you can create it, and your tools are your imagination and your emotions—passion, actually.

Because we are multidimensional beings, we have the ability to create in several, if not many, different realities. We aren't just limited to the physical world anymore. Truly we never were, but we just weren't able to expand our minds to be able to see that. We had no frame of reference. The past is gone, taking with it all thoughts of playing small. You have found that magic lamp, and you aren't limited to just three wishes—you can have as much (or as little) as you can handle.

This book is a toolbox, filled to the brim with ideas to help you get outside the box of your pre-conceived notions and limiting beliefs. It's our hope that you will take a little from each of the contributors and play in their reality as you craft your own methods of conscious creation that work for you—fast, with consistency, ease, and grace!

As you move through this book you will find that there is a consistent thread—choice. In every moment you are creating. WHAT you create is your choice.

As our consciousness increases, more possibilities unfold before us, so please just keep asking bigger questions, open-ended ones. Keep reaching for the stars, because they aren't as far away as they might appear.

Deep love,

Jean Adrienne

PREFACE

This book came about as a co-creation between all of our Realities of Creation Tele-summit speakers. When Jean and I were guided to launch the tele-summit, we were also guided to co-create this book. Our guides simply told us that while the audio was nice, people needed the written word—for the written word expands to others in ways that the spoken word does not. All speakers contributed a chapter on their area of expertise topic—topics that they have been writing about and teaching for a while.

What makes this book so powerful is it contains the energy of nine. Nine is the number of completion. It provides a complete compendium of thoughts and ideas to assist the reader in successful conscious creation. We have nine authors, and any time one or more is gathered, the results are exponentially increased. Each chapter gives you a taste of each speaker, with tips and hints for things you can do right now to implement the topic tools. If any particular author resonates more with you, you can always find more information on that topic from their websites.

In this book you will find:

- Jean Adrienne: *DNA Reality of Creation*

- Leslie Amerson: *Emotional Mastery—Emotional Freedom*
- Julia Griffin: *The True Presence—Your True Self*
- Laurie Huston: *Power of the Heart*
- Linda Minnick: *Perspective*
- Kathleen O'Keefe-Kanavos: *Dreams during The Age of Aquarius*
- Maureen St. Germain: *How To Get a Higher Self-Connection*
- Suzanne Strisower: *You Have a Multidimensional Life Purpose*
- Lynn Waldrop: *The Body-Mind Connection*

Each chapter contains fresh, new information that is coming forth as answers to our questions of why, how, and questions for now. Our reality is changing as we move closer to ascension, and many practices from the past are no longer working. This book provides new information to assist you in your own path of conscious creation.

It is our heartfelt desire that we provide information for you that changes your reality and guides you gently down your own path of self-mastery. We are all in this together. This is the era of collaboration and cooperation. If we can collectively provide you with as little as one nugget, we have done our job, and we only ask that you then pass it on. Make a difference in the world as only you can—with your own unique message.

With hugs, great love, and much appreciation,

Leslie Amerson

DNA REALITY OF CREATION

Jean Adrienne

"The blueprints for the construction of one human being requires only a meter of DNA and one tiny cell . . . even Mozart started out this way."

—L.L. Larison Cudmore

We don't completely understand our DNA. Science has one idea of what it is, metaphysicians have another, and quantum physicists still another. None of these groups fully grasps the whole of what it is. Science even calls the majority of it "junk."

I'm going to offer up my theories for you to ponder—take what you want and leave the rest. Let's start with some "what ifs." What if there is a whole lot more to DNA than we have ever considered? What if your DNA holds all the knowledge that has ever existed? What if DNA is capable of manifesting change—even changing itself? What if DNA has its own intelligence? What if DNA has a *soul*? Let's consider each of these questions separately, come up with hypotheses about them, and then you can reach your own conclusions!

One thing is certain, DNA is more powerful than we know, and we have a lot to learn from and about it. It's the basic building block of life. It allows our cells to reproduce, and maintains the integrity of our species (and all species).

Some years ago, my guides told me that we originally had many more strands of DNA than the two we have presently. The story I was told was that we started out with 144 strands of DNA, and the human containing them was meant to be immortal, allowing unlimited time for the soul to explore every possible reality that can be achieved in a body. I believe this is what was referred to in the Bible when Adam and Eve lived in the Garden of Eden. At some point in our evolution, we gave up DNA—my guides say we did this to assist another civilization from another star system that was dying. These beings came to Earth, bred with us and left, going back home stronger and with the ability to survive. When they left, we had two strands of DNA, not 144, and for all intents and purposes, we have been fine since that time. We have grown in consciousness and even changed physically as a part of our human evolution.

What we didn't realize when we gave up that genetic material out of compassion was that there was an attribute of Christ consciousness associated with each strand of DNA. We gave away some of our gifts and abilities, unwittingly, when we helped the other star beings. This is something we still tend to do, even today. We give to others without looking at the big picture to see the impact or the consequence of this action.

Throughout time there have been humans who have been born with all 144 strands intact. Jesus is an example, but there have been others in various civilizations around the planet and in other times. Jesus had access to all his gifts and abilities, and he was eager for us to realize that we could, too, because nothing is really lost in the divine plan. All we have to do is ask and intend and we can find anything we have lost. That's part of the divine promise.

What if there is more to our DNA than we have ever considered?

Science has examined the human genome and has assigned meaning to less than half of it. The rest, they have deemed "junk." We've all heard the saying, "God didn't create no junk . . ." so it seems pretty restrictive to me that science would dismiss such a large portion of our DNA as such. If we could make use of this remaining DNA, there is no limit to what we might be able to create. Studies show that people who are close friends have similar DNA. A good example of this is how people who have been in relationship for a long time begin to look like each other. Facial characteristics are DNA derived, so it's possible that our DNA changes over time based on association.

We now know that attention and intention can create, so why not put our intention on our DNA and intend that change take place? I believe that this is the portal to potential going forward. If we can harness this energy, we can heal our bodies from the DNA out. We can youth and regenerate to whatever level we desire. We can release inherited patterns, changing negative to positive, and so much more! This is a holographic universe. If we have souls, and I think we agree that this is a truth, then every cell of our bodies has a soul. Within every cell is a nucleus containing chromosomes containing DNA, so each of these must have souls as well. Since we have a soul purpose, there must be a purpose all the way

3

down to the DNA level and more. It's time for us to begin this work of unification and cooperation with all our parts, so that we can achieve at the level we were intended.

What if your DNA holds all the knowledge that ever existed?

I believe it does. We've been taught to think this knowledge is outside us—in akashic records, somewhere. My belief is that the akashic records exist in our very DNA. Masters throughout time have stated that the kingdom of God lies within us, so why would we look for our answers anywhere else?

Our DNA is sentient. We can communicate with it. The answers always come when we go into the silence and ask. Where do you think they come from?

If you can access all the knowledge that ever existed (and I believe you can) there is no problem too large for you to solve. The only question is where to begin!

What if DNA is capable of manifesting change—even changing itself?

We have already begun to look at this in one of the earlier questions, so let's take it to the next level. Genetically this is called evolution, but when we add consciousness into this equation, we have *conscious evolution*—positive change using attention and intention. Soon we will do experiments to validate these theories, but for now let's look at how this can happen. When we use attention and intention in conjunction with our DNA, we are actually *recruiting* it to assist us.

Just like building an army, the more DNA we have access to, the more players there are to support our desired changes. This is where locating all our DNA comes in to play, and once that's been done, using all of it to create the changes we desire.

4

What if DNA has its own intelligence and its own soul?

Back to the holographic universe—it HAS to. Since it is a part of you, it must be in alignment with your soul and your soul's purpose, even if it has its own soul and purpose. Let's face it—we are in it together!

If we agree that this is possible, that DNA is a sentient component of YOU, once again, it only makes sense to communicate with it. One of the biggest mistakes we make as humans is to assume that others know what we want. Assumption is one of the reasons we haven't had access to the power of our DNA before now. We just assumed it was biological "stuff" and never asked it to help us! Crazy! Why *wouldn't* it help us?

You are a multidimensional being, and your DNA is multidimensional as well. What's really cool about this are a couple of things. We are generally aware of only one of the dimensions in which we operate. Depending on how far down this rabbit hole you have already gone, some of you might be aware of more than one, but for the purpose of this discussion, let's agree that we consciously operate in one dimension. As a multidimensional being, however, there are many more aspects of *you* running around doing other things in other places. Sometimes these aspects actually help you, even without your being aware that they have. Let me share an example.

Most people know me as a healing facilitator, and I get a lot of calls from folks in crisis asking for my assistance. It isn't always convenient for me to drop what I am doing to dive into their situation and work with them. One afternoon, I received such a call while I was driving. I told the man that I would be happy to work on him when I got back to my office, in several hours, and he thanked me. An hour later he called again. He said, "I could feel you working with me about twenty minutes ago, and when you were done, all the pain was gone—and it hasn't returned. Thank you SO much!" Of course, I couldn't tell him how surprised I was to hear this, because I hadn't actually done anything (consciously). But some aspect of me did, that's for sure.

This is just one example, but this sort of thing happens to me a lot! Think of how much more you can accomplish when you actually ASK all your aspects in every dimension, AND all your DNA to support you in achieving everything you desire to achieve and manifest in your life!

Practical Applications

Now for the fun part. We will locate and activate latent strands of DNA and enlist them to assist us in creating every-thing we desire! We have nothing to lose and a lot to gain. This can be done by using your attention and intention, which are your tools for manifestation in this new reality. To support you in this I will provide you with ten energetic glyphs, drawings that hold the frequency of these latent strands of DNA, so that you have a focal point for your attention, and then you can use your intention to actually activate them.

Jesus said, "I came that you should have life, and have it abundantly." He didn't say anything about loss, poverty, lack, pain or suffering. He lived this aspect of consciousness. Everything he required was provided for him, at exactly the moment it was needed. He walked in complete faith and trust that this would be so.

Where did we get so far off track? When did we internalize the belief that there wasn't enough to go around? Like so many of the limiting beliefs we have picked up over time, it doesn't really matter where or when we learned this, only that it isn't part of our soul makeup. Waking up to that point is the beginning of truly living here on Planet Earth. Until we accept this first basic tenet, fear still has the option of gaining a foothold in our lives.

Let's talk about fear for a moment. It slips into our awareness like water through a crack, and undermines our foundation until our entire reality falls into a sinkhole. It happens quickly, literally like a thief in the night, stealing our peace. Before we know it, it has consumed us, and as we have learned from the Law of Attraction, what we focus on is what we create, so fear begets more fear until we are paralyzed, stopped frozen in our tracks and unable to see clearly that it is just an illusion. Fear is the illusion and abundance is our birthright.

There is a reason that this glyph is the first one we examine. Your external reality is a reflection of your internal landscape. When you place your reference points for safety, security and success outside yourself, you look for your abundance in the external. The source of all abundance is in your connection to Creator God. It is unlimited.

Abundance is a frequency, a vibration of energy, and unless you hold the energy of abundance within you, it can't be magnetized to you in the outer world.

With this activation you pull all your reference points back to your Divine Connection to Source and away from money, relationships, job, family, "stuff" or anything outside of you. Feel the freedom you just created for yourself!

Compassion is an empathetic resonance. When we are in this vibration, we support another without falling into alignment with their vibration. This, in turn, allows us to assist them in raising their own vibration. We can't do this

COMPASSION

for someone else. Vibrational shift is a very personal thing; it happens through personal responsibility and accountability alone, contrary to popular thought.

Sympathy is another empathic resonance. We are all familiar with this one. When we go into sympathy, we connect deeply into the emotion of another, and this can create a drain on our own energy. We have an innate desire to help others, especially when another person experiences a loss, but giving your energy or power to them not only doesn't help, but can also slow their own healing. It's a form of enabling actually.

A healthier way to assist another is to give them your attention and compassion and then model right energy of healing and processing for them. Do this at the level of the Higher Self. In this manner there is no energetic entanglement.

We are unique aspects of the Divine Mind. As such, we have access to all knowledge. Just like the aspect of connection, there isn't any limit to what we know. In fact, everything that has ever been experienced or learned is part of this repository of conscious knowledge.

So why do some of us appear to be smarter than others? It relates to our level of connection into consciousness.

Unfortunately, this aspect has been more deeply hidden than some of the others. This doesn't mean that it's harder to access, just that we have to become more awake to realize it's there.

The great mystery schools throughout the ages were dedicated to achieving this connection for the initiates, and there was concern that having access by the masses would lead to danger and abuse. In today's vibration, however, the time for secrets is well past, and the tools for accessing Consciousness are readily available to those who look for them. This book is an example of one of these tools. By working with these glyphs and activating all your DNA and the associated attributes of consciousness, you are tapping into the oldest and deepest knowledge. Make it your own!

Being the Creator implies a LOT of responsibility! In fact, it's such a scary thought that most of us deny our own truth.

It's a lot easier to blame somebody else when things don't look like we expected or wanted them to!

This attribute of consciousness goes back to the truth that we are unique aspects of the one Creator Source. So, that means that we aren't the ONLY creators out there. There are lots of us working our individual magic in the field of potential.

Here are a couple of rules that govern creation, because it's easier to play the game when you know the rules.

- You can't create in the reality of another. You are only responsible for creating your own. Another way of looking at this rule is "mind your own business." Allow everyone else to be responsible for taking care of themselves.

- You are accountable for the things you create. Just like Great Creator tends to the flowers, animals and sea creatures, you have to tend to your own garden. This is done by being conscious in your creations— using your attention and intention wisely.

- It's always smart to be open to suggestion from a higher source when creating, so when you place your intention onto the Universe, add, "This or something better is mine now, thank you!" By doing so you open the door for God to give you even more than you might have asked for.

This consciousness attribute walks hand-in-hand with surrender. We can only attain true freedom when we fully release our attachments to everything (anything and anyone). This can

only be accomplished by fully surrendering to the will of Spirit.

It's so counterintuitive! Every time I have thought I let everything go, I found there was at least one more thing I was holding on to. Every time I asked the Universe to provide for me, but doubted or questioned and didn't get the response I expected, it just put another nail in the coffin I was building for myself.

Only recently, with this activation, have I come to know that the only way to be free is to fall into it—just like the term *free fall.* The feeling is amazing. All sense of weight goes away. Just about the time I would have fallen into fear, an updraft, like a thermal wind current, catches me and lifts me higher than I have ever been before.

The view from this place is spectacular! Freedom allows you to see clearly, to understand the cause and effect of all actions—yours and others. It gives you the power to choose freely, because you can clearly see all the possibilities and potential outcomes to your choices.

All the things we held onto are neutral now, making it easy to let them go. What could be so important as to allow it to stand in your way to ascension?

We were never meant to age and die—we began this game of life as a game of immortality. Somewhere along the way we forgot this, unfortunately, hence the cycle of karma and the struggle we took on to be our lot in life. This activation returns you to your divine blueprint at the cellular level. The glyph looks interestingly enough like one of the proteins the body uses to maintain itself. When you receive this attribute, you also activate this particular protein to do its job, and the cycle of life punches the restart button!

Each of your cells is waiting for you to call out to it at the soul level and invite it to return to the immortal state that exists deep in cellular memory, buried through thousands of incarnations, wounding and loss. It's like a seed that's been planted waiting for spring to warm it so that it can sprout. Your cells rejoice when they are set free from the old patterns that always end in death.

Try this: Call out to the souls of every cell in your body and ask that they replicate in their individual truth back to their divine blueprint. Go inside yourself and listen as they sing in harmony with the frequency of love. Feel the joy, the bliss at a cellular level and watch as miracles occur within your physical vessel.

Freedom is our right, but how many of us really feel free? Why is that? Nobody to blame but ourselves. Over time we have taken responsibility for the lessons and issues of others. We have not accepted things that happened to us, stuffing the pain and holding it in our bodies and fields. We have hurt ourselves and others and held onto the guilt. Basically we have weighed ourselves down with dense energy to the point that we have lost the grasp of who we are and what we came here to do.

This activation releases you from all that you have taken on so that you can open to the possibility that there is more that you can be. But it does even more—it releases everyone else you have connected to as well. Think about all those you have judged. Every judgment creates a reference point to that person, and now those connections are being released like balloons, up and off of you.

Liberation is about relationship, the relationship between you and you, you and others, and you and God. In the light of the new reality, we are learning to be responsible and accountable for our thoughts, words and actions, and therefore going forward, we will create much less pain for ourselves as a collective.

We ARE multidimensional beings. It's time for us to get used to this. I believe that there are a finite number of dimensional aspects to our souls. I'm just not sure what that number is—perhaps 144 since that seems to be a very common number within sacred geometry.

While each of these aspects is a facet of our one soul, we aren't all exactly alike. We are part of the same consciousness, but the difference is how conscious each aspect is—what experience it has lived, perhaps where. Some of our aspects may be incarnate on Earth, some may not be incarnate at this particular time, and many are in differing dimensions. But because they are a part of a whole, they can be aligned to support their other aspects.

Until now we had no idea that there was any part of us that wasn't this one. But with our new awareness comes greater potential! This activation prepares you to call out to all your other aspects and ask for help with anything that concerns you. This is accomplished with attention and intention, just like everything else in this new reality.

For example, you have a daunting task in front of you—one that you don't think you can pull off. Perhaps you need to create a website for your new business, but have never had any training in web development. So, ask that all your aspects align with you. Then ask that an aspect that has experience in web development step up and share their knowledge and experience in this area with you and give thanks. Now wait . . . your response to this

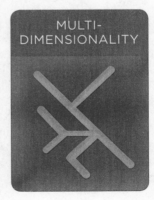

request may take many forms. You might just know where to go to find the appropriate, self-explanatory software to help you. Or, you might get an email from a web development coach offering their services. Remember—one of the cardinal rules of manifestation is that "how" is not your job, so let go and allow!

Every cell of your body has a soul, and each of those souls are on your team. They support you in being all you can be. This activation allows you to call out to your team to return to the divine blueprint of perfect health and well-being for your physical body. This vessel was created to house your soul essence in a manner that would allow you to be your best and accomplish everything you choose. Don't settle for less than that.

What this activation actually does for you is to return each cellular component back into phase with perfection, opening

the way for you to claim it, to align with it, and to manifest your body to the point where you are the most comfortable.

Try it now. Call out to the souls of all your cells. Invite them to align with you in creating perfection in your body—perfect health, perfect vision, perfect weight! Breathe and feel what happens next. Enjoy it! Be IN JOY with it! LOVE your BODY!

We can't begin to love another until we first understand what it means to love our self. This love must be free from stipulation, free from conditions, and free from judgment in every way.

Our soul job here on Earth is to learn about love. Where we come here from, there is only love, but those memories are put away during our time in these bodies, and we live in the illusion that we are separate from that love, from God and from everyone else. We learn to deal with people, places and situations that  push us in the opposite direction from love so that we can figure out what love really is. Once we begin to wake up from this dream of separation, we begin to realize that love is what we are. For some of us it's taken many lifetimes to get here.

So, all we are is energy, and that energy is love. This pure essence resides in the body, but is not the body. And our task is to maintain the integrity of what we are—pure love—and release everything else.

EMOTIONAL MASTERY— EMOTIONAL FREEDOM

Leslie Amerson

"Each of us makes his own weather, determines the color of the skies in the emotional universe which he inhabits."
—Bishop Fulton J. Sheen

Emotions . . . This is an interesting word and it conjures up all kinds of feelings. Through the years, it has been given a bad rap and has been used negatively any time someone else wanted control or didn't want to deal with their own bad behavior. You know—all those times someone said, *"Don't get emotional on me," "Check your emotions," "Watch your emotions," "Don't be so sensitive; I was only joking," "You're over-reacting," "Don't be such a cry baby,"* and my all-time favorite, *"Stop acting like a girl."* Really?

Emotions are tricky, slippery, often messy and sometimes can appear to trip us up—*all the time.* Emotions are complex and a major part of who you are. We all know about our physical body as we see it every day. However, the rest of us consists in ways we cannot "see" but "see" the effect. For example, our mental body is where our thoughts and ideas come from. Some like to say that is the brain. Our spiritual body is that part of us that is sometimes called soul, essence, particle of God, Higher Self, or higher consciousness. Our emotional body is the part of us that stores all of our feelings. All of these "bodies" make up something I like to call the *tapestry of you*, and they are bodies we cannot see with our physical eyes.

What do tapestries all have in common? They are woven, one thread at a time up and down and side to side, often with multiple colors and textures to create a form and image. You can cut a few threads and the tapestry will start to age and look worn. You can pull a thread and it will distort or begin to unravel. No single thread is the master—all threads are important, interact with each other, depend on each other, and together they make a one-of-a-kind tapestry—just like you.

So let's look deeper into our emotions. Emotions are that state of consciousness where we experience the inner and outer world coming together. Examples of these are love, joy, bliss, happiness or sorrow, anger, fear, guilt, shame, embarrassment, humiliation, etc. Emotions are different from our cognitive and volitional states of consciousness. They can and do affect our physical body—we can feel sad, and the body will produce a tear; we can feel fear, and our hearts will race, we might start shaking or trembling, we might run, we might strike out, or yell or scream. Emotions can and do affect our mental body as well. We feel love, and all we can think is how beautiful and wonderful something or someone is. We feel anger, and all we can think is how awful something or someone is.

When we think of our own tapestry, every spoken word, every visual image, every sound, every color, every smell, every touch all create a physical, mental, emotional impact on our body. The degree of the impact is determined by the intensity. For example, a wreck, a robbery, or a rape all have very intense negative impacts. Seeing a baby for the first time, falling in love, or seeing a sunrise, sunset or rainbow all have very intense positive impacts. Background noise like traffic, lawn mowers, and refrigerator hums all have fairly neutral impacts.

Life experiences become different for each of us, based on our own tapestry. They are colored by our daily experiences, our upbringing and family, our teachers, friends, beliefs and dispositional attitudes. They are shaped by our ability to reason, problem solve, and our exposure to events happening around us.

This is why when I say the word *skunk*, everyone has a different response—physically, mentally, and emotionally. If you have never encountered a skunk, you are probably very neutral. If you have had a negative experience with a skunk, like when your cat got sprayed by a skunk and had to be bathed and wasn't allowed in the house for three weeks, you probably have a stronger impact, because the intensity is different in a negative. If you have had a positive experience, like riding in a wagon at sunset with your grandpa and smelling a skunk in the woods as you passed, you probably have a stronger impact because the intensity is different in a positive way. This same principle applies to all things. Why?

When we have a thought or idea, we ponder it. Then we add the five senses to it—see it, hear it, touch it, taste it, smell it—each action has a level of intensity. Then we start to feel it with a greater intensity. When we add our beliefs, attitudes, opinions, and past experiences to it, everything starts to shift up and down the intensity scale. Then color and sound get added and another thread or two is added to your tapestry. As we get older, our dispositional attitudes, opinions and beliefs grow in intensity; they lock into our physical body cells and into our emotional body, and then they "flavor" everything that comes next. And here's the really crazy part—they will flavor our experiences without our conscious awareness or discernment for whether it has any truth or real bearing on the subject!

So, then what exactly *is* emotional mastery and freedom? Much as the words imply, mastery of the emotional body comes by really grasping what is at the root of all your emotional imprinting on any given subject and then choosing how you want to respond every time, rather than responding by habit or negative programming. Freedom comes from choice and awareness. You see, every experience is creating an imprint on your tapestry. It is the level of intensity that is locking it into your cells and subconscious, and to master it and be free from it is to release that intensity from your cells and subconscious so that you can view every past experience from a place of neutrality or positivity so that all future experiences are different and can come from a place of calm, peace, love, compassion, joy, and happiness.

Sounds simple enough, right? The principles *are* very simple. Mastery requires the willingness to create change and daily application so that it becomes your habit and way of life. Freedom comes when you cannot be impacted negatively by your external world.

Okay, so now what? Well, let's start with some questions . . . because we all know that you can never provide an answer when the question was never asked.

Let's recap—so far we have covered what emotions are, how we get them, how and why they impact us. Now let's go deeper.

When you were conceived, you became aware of your parents' and other family members' attitudes, beliefs, life experiences, and what was going on in the world at that time. This awareness began its imprinting on your tapestry. All the joy and happiness or worry, fear and sadness began making its mark on your attitude, opinions and beliefs. Until you turned two years old, you didn't even know you were a separate being from your parents or primary care taker and you took on, were imprinted, by everything they were carrying. All that belief, worry, and joy has been imprinted in your physical body cells, your emotional body, as well as your mental body, and is occupying the driver's seat for all future experiences! Here's where choice and free will enter the picture. You either accepted all this programming and are repeating it, or you rebelled against it and chose differently for yourself. This is also why you might align and agree in some areas and resist and rebel in others, creating a unique one-of-a-kind tapestry of you.

Growing up empathic, my aunt used to call me *that peculiar child*. As a child, I didn't know what that meant. I did know that it didn't feel nice, kind or loving and she was judgmental, mean and fearful—an impact to my tapestry. It wasn't until I was older that I began to understand. I have always, simply "known things," and to my aunt, having a child that was so aware frightened her, mostly because she came from a time when adults "knew everything" and children didn't or couldn't possibly. Today, we have a completely different awareness of what our children come in knowing, and back then, it was unusual for many.

As I became a teenager, I got into playing with words and seeing how they "felt" to me. I made it a fun game to read the word, speak the word, feel the word, and then I would look up the word and see if the socially recognized definition was a match to what I was feeling. Later, I began to sense the color and sound of the words.

This all led me on a quest to focus on the words that were associated with our emotions. In the simplest of terms, I found love and everything that is not love. I noticed all the words we use to define the degrees of how far we are from love—dislike, disgust, revolting or frustrated, irritated, pissed, angry, rage. However, we have one word—*love*—that we use to describe all of our positive and caring emotions for everyone and everything. I love my parents, I love my siblings, I love my children, I love my significant other, I love myself, I love my body, I love my dog, I love my cat, I love my ferret, I love my birds, I love my rabbits, I love water, I love flowers, I love the sunset, I love the sunrise, I love my car, I love my house, I love my job, and I love my financial freedom. We all know that we *feel* the difference in the love we feel for all the people, places and things, but we use only one word. Yes, sometimes people will use the word *like*; however, I find that the word *like* fits better as a variation of happiness and joy.

What I discovered was when our love is anything other than pure unconditional love, it is because we have included another *non-love* emotion, belief, opinion or dispositional attitude into our tapestry, and it is running consciously or mostly subconsciously. For example, if your parents or primary caretaker as a child had a dislike or distrust for other people because of their ethnicity, gender, financial status or position, or as a result of a personal experience, you have added that to your tapestry with the intensity that it was given to you. Intensity in this case can range from constant chatter or create an intense event that was traumatic. In all cases, it is flavoring your tapestry and every experience and thought you have had since.

Here's a little game you can play to see what I'm talking about. Get a piece a paper and draw two lines top to bottom so you have three columns. Label them Negative, Neutral and Positive. Down the side start listing words that relate to people, animals, places, things and events. And yes, you may need more than one piece of paper. I actually filled three notebooks when I first did this. Next, look at each word, take a breath and ask yourself, how does this feel to me, and place a mark in the appropriate column where you think you are feeling. This is your first indicator of where you need to focus your attention for emotional mastery and emotional freedom. As a general rule, anything positive or neutral toward positive doesn't require work right now, the exception being if your word test was something very negative such as rage or killing or revenge or harming others. If you feel very strongly about that, this is an entirely different session and requires more in-depth work.

So we now have a list of words and we kind of know how we feel about each one. Let's explore an example you can use for each one that is invoking a neutral toward negative or negative response for you.

If you have a neutral toward negative or negative response for a parent or primary caretaker, let's dig deeper and excavate the emotions you have locked into your body cells that are flavoring your emotions.

Ask yourself how much you are feeling each of these emotions when you think of that person: sadness, fear, guilt, shame, anger, rage, embarrassment, and humiliation and rank each one on a scale of 1 to 10 with 1 being a little and 10 being a lot.

For any one that you scored 5 to 10, dig deeper. This may take a bit to uncover because you want to go back to the very first time you felt the emotion and then get a feel for how often you continued to feel it.

For example, if you found that fear scored a 9 on your scale, and it began when you were three years old because your parent or caretaker was abusive (physically beat you, molested you, was hateful, mean, and made you feel unloved and unwanted, etc.) check to see what that set up for you.

Did it make you withdraw, feel unsafe, try to be a good girl or boy, not make waves, become invisible, rebel, start fights, or become aggressive, etc.? Next, look back at your list at all the other neutral toward negative and negative word responses you have and see how many of them come from this one incident.

There is no need to dig deep here with the other words, because I'm going to show you how to clear them all quickly without spending days going down memory lane on each one. It is important to do one to three of them just so you can cognize the process and see for yourself the impact on you, and then we will turn it into a protocol to work effortlessly and quickly on the others.

The next step is to discover where your mental body, physical body, and emotional body are storing these emotions. Yes, all three will lock it in, and yes, all three may lock it into a different body part and/or organ and gland system.

You will want to ask the mental body, physical body, and emotional body separately, where did it store the fear of the parent or caretaker (from our example above—you will use the emotions from your own example)? Was it in your: Brain? Heart? Stomach? Legs? Feet? Arms? Hands? Other body part?

If you are like most of us, the results may surprise you. When I did this exercise, my personal fear of my father was locked into my emotional body heart, my physical body arms and hands, and in my mental body feet. So I had stored fear of father figures, figures of authority and/or men into all three bodies but in different areas! The impact on my tapestry has shown up in different ways, in different body parts, every time I encounter father figures, figures of authority and/or men. Depending on the interaction and experience, a different part of my body would respond and loop that around to all the other bodies, locking it into my cells and weaving another part of my unique tapestry!

LET'S RECAP—you made your list of words, you found your personal emotional scale relative to each one, and you chose one to unravel. You dug deeper into the emotion, found the start point and what it invoked for you, and then where you stored it in your bodies—mental, physical and emotional. Then you glanced at the other words to see which ones were affected by this one single imprint.

Now, this imprinting most likely occurred when you were a child, and for many, it is completely running in the subconscious mind. As an adult, you are aware you have fears, biases, opinions, judgments and dispositional attitudes and can now see how some of them formed as a result of this one thing.

As an adult you have a totally different perspective than you did as a child. As a child you were vulnerable, impressionable, and didn't have the cognitive skills you have today. So what do we do?

First, do a meditation, guided or unguided, to that sacred heart space, and find that inner child who was wounded.

Talk to that little child, make them feel safe, loved, wanted and protected. Hold them, laugh, and let them know they are cherished and that you'll come back.

Second, sit down and talk to your bodies—physical, mental and emotional—to let them know that you as your Higher Self are here and in charge. Here's the funny part. Your mental body has been thinking that it is in charge whereas your physical and emotional bodies view the mental body as a sibling. No wonder they fight and don't get along! Once you have established that you (your Higher Self) is indeed in charge, and release the mental body from all responsibility, then you can deal with them as children who want to be heard. As you ask each one how they feel and why, and you listen, they will start to release the "hold" where they locked the charge into the body. The point is to listen to them individually. Once they trust that you (your Higher Self) are in charge and that you will listen to them, then they can find the forgiveness that is required from the adult perspective. As you help them each feel safe, they will let go of the emotional charge that has locked it into the body.

This is how we begin to unravel the negative impacts of your emotions on your mental, physical and emotional bodies. You really only have to do a few of them so that each body gets it, and when they release the lynchpin of the stuck emotion, many, many, many others automatically unravel because they came from the lynchpin emotion! How cool is that?

You will know you are successful when something that used to trigger you comes back around and you have zero emotional charge. When you can acknowledge that it has zero emotional charge, it will go away and you will have emotional mastery over that.

If, on the other hand, something that used to trigger you comes back around, you look at it, and all that emotion comes flooding back, then you haven't completely let it go, and at that moment, you re-lock it all right back into your cells. Oh, crap!

So what is this telling us? That there is something deeper going on—we haven't found the original source lynchpin and/or we weren't really ready to let it go.

Why? Sometimes our beliefs become cherished. A cherished belief is something we have picked up along the way and made it a governing factor from which we base our entire existence—whether it is founded in truth, and most of the time it is not.

Where do cherished beliefs come from? They come from our parents, our teachers, our preachers, our friends, our lovers, the news, books we read, our children and our life experiences. They show up in our opinions, views and dispositional attitudes, and they flavor our unconditional love toward all things. They become cherished when we discount another person's contradictory view, opinion or attitude. We will become defensive or angry when our cherished belief is being "challenged." All this is really telling you is that inner belief is in conflict with your outer experience. What you do about it is totally and completely up to you. Do you see it as invalid or as an opportunity for growth? Are you really ready to let it go and choose something that is in alignment with truth and unconditional love, or are you enjoying it way too much? There is no right or wrong answer here—only an individual choice for what you are choosing for your life and your unique tapestry. You are one-of-a-kind. This is your life to live according to your rules and no one else's.

Here's another caveat: you have to want to let go of your cherished beliefs and dispositional attitudes for any clearing work to take place, and a lot of this work is going to bring them up and you may not yet be ready to let go. That's okay; when you are ready, you will. There is no judgment; it isn't a race. It is only a *choice* to have emotional mastery and freedom.

Emotional mastery is about your desire to see what's going on in your life, decide what you want to change, and then take the action steps to change them and live by those changes. It is about being unflappable when there is chaos around you. It is about loving someone who has committed a perceived wrong against you. It is kindness, forgiveness, respect, honor, integrity and love—unconditionally.

Emotional mastery is an individual choice. Our emotions are simply indicators that tell us where we need to work on ourselves, where we are stuck, have hang-ups and are operating from a place other than unconditional love. It shows us all the ways where we have added something else to our soup.

Consider this: negative emotions are like feces or dog turds. Would you eat a bowl of soup that had a few dog turds floating in it? They are small and only one of twenty ingredients; they don't make the soup smell bad. So would you consume the soup? What if I spread the dog turds on bread with honey? Would you consume it then? I know this is graphic, and it is to make a point. No, you most likely wouldn't consume the soup or the sandwich, so think about how you are mentally "consuming" negativity into your body—consciously or unconsciously through words, actions, deeds, thoughts, beliefs, behaviors, opinions, judgments, and dispositional attitudes. If you can mentally tell yourself that all negative emotions are like dog turds, then you can "see" how they are tainting your senses, your emotions, and your thoughts, and then you can change them.

Emotional *freedom* comes when we no longer go to that place of blame, shame, guilt, anger, intimidation, etc. It comes when we have emptied out all of the opinions, judgments, and points of view that were never ours to start with, and start living our lives from a place of wonder. When we no longer have triggers that take us to a dark place, we can stay in a joyful and happy place. When we are no longer affected by circumstances we cannot change, we can then look for a different possibility.

You have gotten only a small taste of what emotional mastery and freedom are and how to achieve it. It doesn't happen with just one action; it occurs with every breath, every thought, every action, and every word. It is a *choice* since we are the only ones that can think and feel for ourselves. We can allow the actions of others to irritate us, but it is *our* action alone that determines the outcome, since it is our choice on how we respond to the outside world.

No one has power over you in any way unless you give it to them, and we train people how to treat us by how we feel about ourselves. We feel about ourselves according to what we have woven into our tapestry. The really awesome thing is—and here's the secret—*you will never finish your tapestry.* You are always a work in process. You can reweave any part of your tapestry any time you choose!

Simply make a choice, give yourself permission, and then just do it! You do not need anyone else's permission. You are as free as you allow yourself to be. You are judge, jury and jailer—or you are liberator. Your choice.

I know it can feel overwhelming, much like trying to eat an elephant. Elephants are huge. The secret is to realize everyone eats an elephant exactly the same—one bite at a time. It doesn't matter where you start—it only matters that you start.

For emotional mastery, you pick one, any one, and you start there. Which one are you ready today to let go? Is it fear? Anger? Embarrassment? Guilt? Shame? Blame? Sadness? Rage? Humiliation? What do you think would serve you the best if you let it go?

Now that you have made a decision, get busy. Revoke its driver's license, remove it from the driver's seat of your life, take the wheel, and drive your own life. It cannot control you if you do not let it. Baby steps, awareness, desire for change, and willingness to follow through is all that it takes. You can do it! Do you realize that simply *deciding* to do it is truly 90 percent of the change? So all the rest is a measly 10 percent. That's it. Ten percent is really *not* that much!

You will find that when you decide to let go of all the emotions that are not love, your life will get better. You will find inner happiness, joy, and be comfortable in your own skin. You will find that you can forgive. Forgiveness is not believing that someone else's actions did no harm or didn't happen. Forgiveness is about releasing it from your body, letting go of the emotional charge and becoming free. Free from the bondage of the pain you locked into your cells. Freedom from the imprinting of the negativity of the circumstances, events and experiences. Freedom to view it as a movie (minus the emotional charge) and to find the growth nugget.

Weaving your own beautiful one-of-a-kind tapestry that is uniquely yours is your only measuring stick to your own personal progress—from where you were before to where you are now. You can never truly compare yourself to anyone else.

We are all individually unique, special and awesome in our own way. Progress is measured in terms of past behavior. For example, if I did that thing I do ten times a day, every day, and then worked on myself and made new habits so that I only did that thing I do one time six months later—WOW! That's progress, and worthy of a gold medal! Can you see it? From ten times a day every day for years to one time one day after six months. Let this be your personal measuring stick.

You are standing at the edge of the ocean, toes in the water, looking out at the horizon, and you have all the water to go. Dream your wildest dream, and then set about to accomplish it. Use your emotions as your compass guide to tweak your journey, and get busy having the best life possible—with emotional mastery and emotional freedom.

THE TRUE PRESENCE—
YOUR TRUE SELF

Julia Griffin

"Let others see their own greatness
when looking in your eyes."
—Mollie Marti

To invoke the True Presence—the True Self—think of the
wave of the ocean, the singing of a stream, the line of the
horizon at sunset, or the first pulse of love. Think of joy, the
union of the body and spirit, the exclamation of the spirit
when one is creative, and the expression of the inner gifts.
There is motion and stillness, a merging of energies beneath
these feelings. The true presence is always there; yet, it merges
with the outer self, the part of the self that experiences physical reality. In many ways, it represents the union between the
inner and outer self. Yet, it is far more than this experience.

Known as alchemical gold, the treasure in the tower, or
the tiny lotus hidden in the heart, the true self is the awakened
part of our being, which eternally resides within us. Our true

presence is connected to the One and the All; it deciphers the sound of flowers, the language of animals, and people. It speaks through the heart. The flow and rhythm of life appeal to us and reveal their mysteries.

The True Presence manifests and creates. It connects us to the divine and flows through our being—if we allow it and/ or beckon to it. It shapes universal energy into the form of our thoughts and heart's desires. It whispers secrets of nature into the ear. The inner presence finds joy in the simplicity of birds, the touch of the wind, or the low pitched speech of trees.

It reads the pulse of energy beneath in animate objects with the heart. It is far more than these descriptions; it is the flame of the heart, the desire of the soul, stillness and peace, quietness and motion. These are fractal glimpses of higher consciousness. Any similar encounter is a response from the true presence. It is simple as a kiss from a child or as complex as the radiation of light or the response of spontaneous healing—the sensation of an alternative universe.

The True Self knows the next step on the path, the methodology of finding a higher frequency, and the right vision for creative urges. It speaks about the light of the soul, communicates with us in moments of despair, and acts as our champion when we step forward on our spiritual journey. The True Self is always there, waiting for our call.

Communication from the True Self is known as the inner voice, a small, still voice, which answers and guides us. (The term "universe" includes the akashic records, the realm of miracles, angels, guides, and the mysteries of the unknown.) Through the True Self, we can connect to the universe at large. Through development of this relationship, we begin to perceive and recognize the energetic resonance of our path. The heart chakra opens and connects with others on our path.

When we are connected to the universal force, it flows through us. It may enhance our intuitive ability or lead us to books, teachers, or opportunities. The universal energy may flow through us with gifts such as clairvoyance, clairsentience, or clairaudience for perceiving the unseen world. It may open our ability to heal, strengthen our body, alter our thoughts, bring in loving relationships, or open us to guidance—as the realization of the components of a higher frequency.

The True Presence leads us into a higher frequency, a wave of higher life. When living in connection with the True Self, we become more aware of negative tendencies, thoughts, and judgments, which remained below the surface in the past. We realize the motion of patterns (repetitive negative events, people, or situations), and we have a strong desire to change our perception of life by moving above the throe of mass consciousness and lower energies on earth. A desire to connect with nature, improve the physical body, and create a new life on the physical plane becomes stronger—as a reflection of the True Presence. Often, we become more aware of the energy of particular objects and/or places, which teaches us about our resonance with life. Note: Spiritual "gifts" can come from the astral as well as spiritual world. It's good to use discernment when reading messages from others by relying on your inner judgment.

A sense of inner knowing and heightened possibility are two of the states which accompany the inner presence. Inner knowing is how we perceive real truth. Some people feel truth with the heart or gut, but it is a palpable feeling—a discernment between realizing truth intellectually or spiritually. As an interesting facet, we become less interested and judgmental about other people's truth and values. We become fascinated by learning the truth that resonates with our inner being. (The Tibetans called this "inborn knowing.")

Recognizing your true self

1. Everyone has had moments of joy, a smooth current of positive happenings in life, strong (correct) intuitions, a sudden knowing of an answer, or unexpected help. A deep connection with nature can also indicate the presence of the True Self as well as a spiritual insight or experience. In a sense, we release the immediacy of the demands of ordinary life and move into a non-ordinary life.

2. The heart speaks to us about the True Self through our deep desires. What attracts us with a sensation of love and heightened spirituality? What gives an energized state and a deeper feeling of connection with the inner presence?

3. Observation is very helpful in finding the True Self. In the morning, spend a few minutes observing the actions of the routine. Observe the self while driving a car. Observe conversations. Who is observing? (Your True Presence observes.) According to quantum physics, when an observer is added to an experiment, the photons change their route. Light responds to an observer. Imagine looking in the mirror. Notice your good qualities. Become aware of your body as you look into the mirror. Imagine you are the person in the mirror, and you are looking at your face and body. Who's observing? Your True Self or True Presence is always observing. It is always there in the totality of your being. There is always a part of you with a loving presence, which is connected to the

universe at large. This part of you is always awake. It
waits for your acknowledgment.

4. We can think about the most illuminated periods
of our lives. By focusing on them, we can recall the
experience of connection. (This is known as the right
use of memories.)

5. A feeling of the "unknown" is often associated with
the True Presence as are love and light. To some
degree, the inner presence is experienced as the
"unknown." Mystery surrounds our journey into light
and love—the auspices of the True Self.

Awakening

Awakening is associated with learning about the True Presence. It is a process, a method of attuning to the direction of
the True Presence. There are several steps of the process. The
first involves believing and knowing the True Self *is* there.
Rest assured that the True Self hears and feels our desire to
know more of it. By recognizing and expanding moments of
connection—such as happiness, peace, or joy—we connect
more deeply.

A feeling of stillness and peace comes with the True
Presence. Meditation develops the feeling of presence. In
meditation, the True Presence mediates between our earthly
presence and the universe at large. It connects us to a larger
paradigm of reality with universal truths, which are much
larger than the laws of "real life." For example, we can send
light or love to a person, without knowing where they are, and
the person can receive it instantaneously. (This is transmit-
tal—a method of sharing one's spiritual truth or abilities.)

One of the indications of success with meditation and
energetic practices is the desire for higher vibrations. The

feeling of universal connection—the True Self—delivers light, expanded possibility, and a deep feeling of love. By culturing and developing this relationship, inner guidance is provided over time.

Awakening is much more than meditating. In my experience, meditation helped in developing an inner calm and a quiet, peaceful feeling. My intuitive abilities also increased. But true awakening came when I saw the inner light in every particle of life. I could see how light lies beneath the structure of every object on the earth—and how the fibers were guided perfectly by the light above. The One Light appeared in many forms. (It's fascinating to note that the inner light of nature responds to our individual light.) Soon after, I found a teacher in wolves—and I learned to see life in a different way.

After awakening, life is the same. But we perceive it in a different light. We become aware of the True Self, which alters our way of understanding life.

In my practice as a teacher, I've watched students experience the process of awakening although their work may have begun with a physical problem such as abundance, relationships, or physical pain. Over time, awakening has come to many of them—and manifested as a deep understanding and ability with universal forces. (It does not come to everyone. Some people simply want to feel better or to have a better life. Others devote themselves to sensing the spiritual energy beneath the practices. But awakening does come to those who seek it with heart, body, and soul.)

1. Everyone has a True Presence. We've all felt it.

2. The True Presence holds the qualities of the soul. It connects us with the universe, the One in All.

3. The level of energy—both physical and spiritual—affects our ability to tap into our True Presence. Higher vibrations help in identifying this presence.

4. Meditation brings about connection with soul qualities. It can increase our light level.

5. All spiritual work is part of finding the True Self.

6. There is a mysterious, unknown quality in spiritual work. We pursue stepping into the unknown.

Exercises for Awakening:

Obviously, awakening is far more than energy, high vibration, or placement of consciousness, but these exercises can help in gaining awareness of your inner self. (I practice all of them at various times—particularly when I desire insight or a shift in awareness.)

ENERGY

Everything is energy. Everything responds to our energy field. The frequency (rate of vibration) of our energy field affects our perception of life. By understanding more about energy, we can move through life with more ease and calm.

1. Notice what gives energy. Think about people, places, and activities. Note the specific feeling they have in common, which will tell you a great deal about yourself.

2. Notice what takes energy. When do you feel tired? What lowers your energy level? What raises your energy level?

3. Pay attention to the energy of the day. When do you have the most energy? When do you feel tired?

It's helpful to rearrange your day (and life) through the above knowledge.

VIBRATION

Energy is measured in vibration. Higher vibration leads to connection with the inner self and higher consciousness.

1. We move into a higher vibration when we experience love, creativity, confidence, and light.

2. A higher vibration can support others by bringing about healing, conscious realization, and peacefulness.

3. We can often vibrate above limitations when we sustain a higher vibration.

We can gain insight by reflecting on our past experiences of holding a higher vibration, or we can imagine the state and how it feels.

HIGHER CONSCIOUSNESS

Higher consciousness is a state of connection, which is always there. We find it through our desire for it—and through practices like meditation, reflection, and self-observation.

1. Everyone is connected. When we focus on connection, we experience more of the state of higher consciousness. We can tap into this several times each day by thinking about it. (How would I feel in a state of higher consciousness?)

2. Pay attention to intuition. Intuition comes from the soul, and we progress more quickly with heightened awareness of our inner "hints." Keep a small notebook for intuition and hunches. Discover the messages from your inner self.

3. Focus on the heart space and unconditional love.

4. Before sleep, relive your day backwards. Recall every event. Make changes and imagine the difficult portions as easy or see it flowing in a different way. (This is a way of pulling the energy of the day back into you as well as revising any patterns.)

A strong desire for higher consciousness, accompanied by small actions and work (above exercises), will activate your progress.

EVOLVING AND AWAKENING

Contact with the True Self often leads to a desire for a continuance of the state of awakening. Our understanding and intimacy with the True Presence develops through our desire to experience more intimacy with the inner self. It becomes the most loving and enlightening method of learning about life. It is more than a spiritual path; it involves balance with both physical and spiritual realities.

Beyond initial awakening, we gain awareness of our ability to create—the way in which life takes on the shape of our consciousness. It's easy to see the passage of light in the areas of life that fall into place easily. We encounter karma or past patterns in areas of difficulty in life. It's best to see these as challenges and continue on our path of evolution. Eventually, the light shows us how to best traverse through the darkness on our path.

If we move back into creating, it's important to know we use the light of the inner presence in manifestation. We actually shape reality into a higher form through our higher consciousness. Everyone creates life through holograms, which are sharp visualizations accompanied by emotion. In the familiar aspects of life, we are so accustomed to creating the holograms that we perform the task automatically. As an example, think of learning to tie a shoe. It's difficult in the beginning, and the task consists of several steps. When we learn the technique, it becomes automatic. We don't think about it.

Much of life runs on "automatic," and we create the events in life without noticing our pattern of thought, emotion, or action. By visualizing our lives in detail, we can create more choices, opportunities, and an entirely new set of emotions, which is based on love—if we invoke the True Self. Recreating life through visualization involves loving ourselves enough to see life differently and to make an effort to create it in a new form.

Another positive aspect of visualization lies in the realization of resistance or the part of the self that creates or resonates with the negativity in our lives. Positive visualization teaches about the negative thoughts and feelings hiding beneath the surface and about resistance to our desire.

Overall, visualization teaches us about discerning the difference between the life we think we want and the life the universe wants for us. Sometimes, these are big lessons. Other times, they are mistakes. (It's the only way of learning the feeling of the right resonance for you.) Creating is one of the most wonderful experiences in life when we manifest through the True Self because we manifest harmony, peace, relief, and contentment—and belief in our self.

Tips:

1. Begin by spending ten or fifteen minutes in meditation each day. Focus on the end result of your desire and hold a happy, pleasant emotion.

2. Over time, your visualization will develop and feel real. If you see signs of manifestation, continue with your work. Reward yourself for small improvements and signs.

3. Begin again when your desire manifests. Soul work involves evolution.

4. Manifestation is not selfish. We are happier when we connect with our True Presence, and we experience the vibrations of the soul when we continue with our work.

5. There is a specific focus with the True Self. Discover how it feels. This is one of the most important aspects of manifestation—finding the relationship with your True Self.

FINDING THE FREQUENCY OF A DESIRE

Everything is frequency. The part of you in the here and now with problems in the day-to-day world holds a specific frequency or set of vibrations. (The set of vibrations makes reality appear as it does. For example, every color or sound vibrates at a specific frequency. Every desire consists of a specific frequency.)

Every problem or pattern reflects a habit of resonance with lower frequency as well as denseness in the physical world or repetition of negative thought and emotion. Solutions are found in higher frequencies or the identification with new vibrations —which are faster and higher than your present problem. Usually people lack the skills to find the images, thoughts and feelings until their vibration lifts through insights, meditations or a big shift.

Over time, I've worked a lot with vibrations, visualizations and frequency. Sometimes, it can feel easier to simply ask for the frequency and the feeling—and then allow the images and actions to flow in on their own, as opposed to creating them. As the energies change, I believe the possibilities will become limitless.

Since we can't possibly know the frequency until we experience it, I've learned to just ask.

Here's the mantra:

Universe, please give me the right frequency so that I can vibrate above this situation. I don't have the answer, but I do want the frequency. Please provide the feeling, visuals and inner guidance to perceive and hold this new frequency.

AWAKENING: THE COLLECTIVE INITIATIVE

It's a special time for awakening. The Precession of Ages, a 26,000-year cycle, along with the turning cycle from Pisces to Aquarius, offers a rare influx of light. Imagine a wheel with spokes. When the spokes are partially closed, we receive a small amount of light. When the spokes are open, the light flows out.

There is an acceleration of time, an amplification of emotion, and a collective energy, which becomes more apparent with the passage of time. The collective awakening occurs among people who understand the workings of light or have an open heart. When the light level of this group grows, it is literally radiated out to the world at large.

For those who are experiencing the dispensation of light (consciously), there is a growing awareness of the ego's internal dialog, the power of light, the collective energy of negative thought, and an understanding of how our personal problems apply to group or world karma. For many, there is a need to retreat from media, crowded locations, and large groups—particularly as we become more attuned on a soul level.

The "shift" amplifies emotions and sensations. We may feel surprised by the depth of our emotions or delighted by our connection with nature. We may find that many of our emotions are hidden beneath social responses. As we drop the mask formed by societal interaction, we find many feelings from adolescence or childhood beneath the surface. It's part of the clearing of old energies from the earth, which are displaced by the new light.

There is also an increasing desire to connect with others who have light and speak positively about life. Many people are becoming more aware of their ability to act as an active creator in life. We understand how every thought or emotion emits a wave—and how the wave spreads through many minds. We are learning how to respond to life with positive visualizations and love as opposed to anger or hate against those who choose to create global problems. We're also learning to visualize and "feel" solutions on the inner plane.

The exciting part of the shift lies in its possibility for finding our power as co-creators. When it becomes necessary to visualize, meditate or observe the self to navigate through life, we quickly develop our skills. For example, if we learn to see life differently and positively, the probability of positively changing our lives and the planet escalates dramatically.

When meditating through spiritual connection on a positive visualization, we automatically hold the frequency for a particular outcome. The current amplification of thought, emotion, and visualization distributes the frequency to anyone who wishes to create a similar reality. Most people with a devoted practice learn the value of sending light to others, projects and world problems because we develop a sincere desire to help.

Sending light and seeing the world differently are probably among the strongest tools to create active change. Let's look at a few personal examples. We can envision projects completed quickly and correctly; we can see success for ourselves and our friends. We can imagine an ample supply of anything we need (including money). All of these states, when practiced with connection, benefit the world because we essentially "send out" the vibration.

A few general examples might include: seeing those who are ill as healthy, the poverty stricken as abundant, and joy in place of sadness. On a global level, we can take several moments each day to see the world with clean water, air and transportation or a fair government.

We can spend our time citing injustices and feeling fear, or we can spend our time creating a new and beautiful world. Like everything, it's a choice. We can spend five minutes criticizing the government or envisioning a better world. The state of the inner self always depends on the choice of placement of consciousness (as does the outer world).

As we come to understand the process of manifestation, it becomes easier to focus on positive thoughts/feelings, and "reality" responds more harmoniously. On the positive side, the world is filled with light workers who are adept at raising their vibration and can quickly change reality by altering their thoughts/feelings or saying a simple prayer.

CONNECTION

Notice the flow. When the physical self is connected with the soul, we experience the True Self. When we connect with the inner presence, we connect with the universe and unlimited possibility. When we connect with our heart's desires, we create them. We also send the frequency of a manifested desire to others who hold light. Light and love connect everything in our universe. When we realize the connection, we awaken.

POWER OF THE HEART
Laurie Huston

"Only do what your heart tells you."
—Princess Diana

We have all heard sayings such as, *Home is where the heart is* and *Follow your heart.* One of my favorite quotes is: "Our Heart carries the wings of our dreams and the desire to realize them," by Fernando Soave.

The heart has the power to deliver our dreams and has been the focus of my energy for several years. I have grown to understand and appreciate this power. Training and research that has proven that my intuitive guidance on the power of the heart is as impressive as I had believed. This chapter has two purposes—one, to show the research that has been done to help you understand the *power of the heart* and how using this research to keep your heart clear and coherent, you may have access to as much of the heart field as possible. Secondly, it is to offer you ways to access the power of the heart to create the dreams you desire in your life and align to your soul's purpose!

The human heart is now documented as the strongest generator of both electric and magnetic fields in the body. This is important, because we've always been taught that the brain is where all of the action is. Multiple Brain Integration Techniques from mBraining.com (research done through Grant Soosla) teaches that we have three brains (proven to date), our mind has 100 billion neurons, the gut brain has 500 million neurons (the same size as the brains of cats and dogs), and the heart has only 30,000-120,000 neurons. While the brain also has an electromagnetic field, it is relatively weak compared to the heart. The heart is about 100,000 times stronger electrically and up to 5,000 times stronger magnetically than the brain. This is important, because the physical world is made of these two fields: the electric and magnetic fields of energy. Physics demonstrates that a change in our electromagnetic field produces atomic level transformation— as we change our energy, we change our state of matter and BEing, and moreover, everyone we encounter. We literally change that atom and its elements within our body and this world. The human heart is designed to do this from an emotional state.

Heartmath.com teaches that our heart emits an electromagnetic field that changes in accordance to our emotions. The magnetic field can be measured several feet from the body. Positive emotions create physiological benefits in your body. You can boost your immune system by conjuring positive emotions. Negative emotions create a nervous system chaos wherein positive emotions do the opposite. The heart has a system of neurons that have both short and long-term memory, and their signals sent to the brain can affect our emotional experience. Our heart sends more information to the brain than vice versa. Our positive emotions help the brain in creativity and innovative problem solving. Positive emotions increase the brain's ability to make good decisions.

What does this mean? The implications are huge!

Research has shown that the heart sends powerful signals to the brain and rest of the body. Once understood and accessed, these heart signals give you more ability to self-regulate your emotions and nervous system and to make changes you thought you couldn't previously make. Throughout history, people have talked about the core values of the heart, which include love, care, appreciation, respect, compassion, kindness, forgiveness and non-judgment. These values and attitudes, which we call core heart feelings, generate the heart signals that bring more coherence to the body's systems. When your initial effort is "from the heart," it brings your mind and emotions into cooperative alignment, and this gives you more intuitive clarity to clear disturbances, and more strength and energy to achieve your goals. That's why coaches say, "play from the heart" or "sing from the heart" or "put your heart into it." Putting your heart into whatever you do gives more power, enjoyment, and better results.

What interferes with our heart's inner power is *stress*. One of the largest positive impacts on stress is through our *breath*. If breath controls the heart, and heart produces our most powerful field generator, then breath becomes one of our most potent catalysts for changing our energy field.

In martial art, yoga, bodywork, counseling, and coaching, we use a tool called entrainment (Heartmath calls *coherence*): a technique for synchronizing and controlling cardiac rhythm by an external stimulus—in most cases, our own breath. As we breathe, so, too, does the entrained individual or group. As we change our breath and entrain others to do so, we change the heart rhythm—the most powerful force in the human body.

However, there are several things that impact our stress levels in a harmful way. Certainly our emotions have a great impact on our stress; some emotions such as boredom or loneliness are often overlooked. Our physical state of being will impact stress; when we have a lack of sleep or exercise, our bodies are affected. Also, our ego/inner critic, etc., impact our level of stress. Learning to become more conscious of how stress is impacting us on a daily level will assist us to make changes in our lives in a positive way and eventually create the life we desire.

Using will power alone never seems to be quite enough to impact the change we desire, as this is a mental activity. It can give you a little momentum, but then it fizzles if there isn't enough heart and emotional commitment behind it. This is because your *heart* brings in the intuitive intelligence and power of your spirit, which is stronger than just trying to discipline your habits from the mind and will power.

Boredom and loneliness

People rarely think of boredom or loneliness as forms of "stress," but they affect heart rhythms the same way that anxiety, depression, and tension do. Both are emotions that people don't often consider to be emotions. They also cover up or "numb" other underlying feelings. Becoming aware of boredom and loneliness as you track your deficit or draining experiences each day, and applying more consciousness will assist you to see what the boredom or loneliness may be numbing. Loneliness is often a sign of a lack of heart connection with one's own self. This program will help you re-establish that heart connection. You will learn how you can work with any emotion or attitude that arises within you, neutralize its charge, and harness its energy to create new positive experiences in your life.

Overcoming insomnia will help reduce stress hormones, balance the nervous system, increase precursors to serotonin, and relax so that you can have more energy to do what you truly desire.

Exercise

Exercise won't take away your reasons for getting stressed, but it strengthens your capacity to manage your stress with less energy loss. You don't have to do a total workout to help clear your thinking and stabilize your emotions. Experiment and find what's comfortable for you, but at least try to get your heart rate up a little for a period of time. Try to be conscious not to replay negative mind loops while exercising. It helps to balance the emotions and calm the mind if you practice the *heart-focused breathing*; it will lower your resistance.

Appreciate yourself—the most valuable investment you can make

Appreciating yourself is a very effective antidote to perfectionism and the inner critic or ego mind. When we activate feel-good feelings in the here and now, and appreciate what you already have, we lower the control and manipulation that our mind/ego wants to create. Comparisons are part of the ego game. When you catch yourself making comparisons or longing for what used to be, find something to appreciate in your life now.

Our *inner critic emotionally sabotages people through perfectionism.* Letting go of trying to be perfect (or giving up when you feel like you're not doing something perfectly) is taking a huge emotional weight off your back. Be kind to yourself as you learn to recognize stress and negative emotions. It is the *inner critic that pulls you out of your feelings and into your head.* See this as a grand adventure, a game, between you and your own heart. Come back to what you are feeling instead, and keep making choices that feel good to your heart. Free yourself from "performing" and keep your attention on your heart, which is non-judgmental, compassionate and gives latitude in the learning process. Each time you let go of performance concerns, self-judgment or guilt, the energy saved will add to your heart power.

Creating a new habit

Researchers at NASA determined that it only takes 21-42 days (3-6 weeks) to create a new habit pattern. The 80/20 rule states that 80 percent of the effort at the beginning yields only 20 percent of the results. At a certain point there is an inversion and you get 80 percent of the results for 20 percent of the effort. In other words, give yourself the gift of knowing that if you continually renew your commitment *for just 21 days,* you've made it through the hardest phase. You are rewiring a neural habit and using the heart to address emotions, which eventually will become second nature. The benefits will reinforce your new habits in an upward spiral, as long as you don't let yourself fall into the trap of giving up and rolling all the way down the hill when you slip. Just pick yourself back up when you fall, and renew your commitment in the here and now. Each time you do this, it counts towards changing your neural habits! You never know which choice will be your tipping point of change.

One of the challenges with changing emotional habits is that the rational part of your brain that learns new things *gets hijacked by the emotions in a stress reaction. It can be frustrating when you have all the best intentions to make new choices and are continually hijacked by old patterns.* It is important to have compassion and understanding for the fact that it is natural to default to old habits, especially under stress. Change can be hard for your body, mind and emotions to adopt a new approach as the default setting right away. The key to making a lasting shift and a neural habit change is *practice* and to apply your tools outside of a stressful context, either in the morning before your day begins or at night when things have quieted down before you go to bed. If you practice the tools in a more controlled environment, they will become second nature after a time, even in the midst of daily stresses. Don't expect this "unconscious competence" right away. Just like driving a car, you will need to think about using your tools for a while, but if you commit to doing them daily, by the end of your program they will become second nature, as your default response to life.

Let's take a look at stressful emotions and how to overcome them:

Step 1: Identify Your Stress Triggers and Stressful Emotions

Which of these areas are likely to provoke stress?

Personal stress
- Self-image
- Self-judgment and guilt
- Relationships
- Health
- Work

- Not enough time
- Other _____

Family stress
- Lack of connection
- Communication issues
- Too many expectations
- Judgments and blame
- Other _____

Friends or Associates stress
- Communication issues
- Too many expectations
- Loneliness
- Boredom
- Other_____

Job stress
- Difficult boss and/or co-workers
- Unrealistic expectations
- Perfectionism
- Feelings of overwhelm (deadlines, priorities, overload, etc.)
- Lack of control
- Judgments and blame
- Other _____

Stress and Emotions

At the core, *all stress is emotional stress* because it affects how people feel. Whether you experience it as mental, emotional or physical stress, if you unmask the word stress, it's about how you feel inside. Stress is registered in your feelings as tension, strain, pain, overwhelm, anxiety, frustration, angst, depression or disturbing undercurrents that you can't find a name for but still sap your energy and leave you feeling exhausted. As these undercurrents occupy your thoughts and feelings, they make it hard to stay with your commitments. We all experience these stressful feelings or attitudes from time to time. It's important to identify the ones you experience often. The following is a list of feelings and attitudes that create stress. Circle the ones that you experience a lot of the time.

- Angry · Depressed
- Bored · Insecure
- Lonely· Perfectionism
- Deprived · Being Judgmental
- Impatient · Resistance
- Irritated · Rebellion
- Frustrated · Guilt
- Worried · Blame
- Anxious · Other

Step 2: Reduce Emotional Stress

You have identified the stressful feelings that can trigger emotional responses from you. Now the next step of this Program is to reduce emotional stress by learning two simple tools that enable you to:

1. Identify your stress triggers as they come up.
2. Redirect your emotional energy.
3. Increase inner security by re-aligning your heart, mind and emotions.

Many people are in denial of or simply unaware of their stress triggers or stress reactions as they are occurring. They may become aware after the fact—after their energy drains, or after a miscommunication, or after physical aches and pains develop, or after they've unconsciously subdued the emotion through distracting themselves. It's important to learn to acknowledge and understand stressful emotions as they come up. These three tools are designed to help you do this.

TOOL #1—AWARENESS AND BEING GENTLE

Awareness and BEing Gentle is a simple yet effective tool for acknowledging emotions. You can learn to release many stressful feelings and stop their energy drain by doing the following simple steps.

1. Notice and admit what you are feeling.

2. Try to name the feeling.

3. Tell yourself to *BE* gentle as you focus on your heart, relax as you breathe, and let the stressful feeling out.

Practice *Awareness and BEing Gentle* at least ten times a day at home, at work, talking on the phone, driving in the car, standing in the line at the store, and so on, just to learn to acknowledge whatever you are feeling. At first, you might not be able to name the feeling. You may think you are feeling nothing. Ask yourself, "Is there tension anywhere in my body?" Ask yourself, "Have I been worrying about anything that may have left a residue in my feelings?" Ask yourself, "Am I feeling peaceful and at ease?" Whatever you are feeling, try to give it a name, acknowledge that you're feeling it, and then add ease to the feeling in Step 3.

Appreciate yourself whenever you can identify and admit what you are feeling. Your feelings aren't bad; they are signals that provide you with information. Stressed or over-stimulated feelings are signals that something is out of balance. Once you acknowledge and accept what you are really feeling, that helps you befriend the feeling, which takes some of the intensity or resistance out of the emotion. As you gently focus in your heart area, relax as you breathe, and let the stress out. This starts to bring your system back to balance.

TOOL #2—POWER OF BEING NEUTRAL

This tool to learn is a simple yet powerful approach for neutralizing and discharging stressful emotions. It's called the *Power of BEing Neutral*. It teaches you to use the power of your heart to bring your mind, emotions and physiology into a more neutral state. Think of Neutral as a "time-out zone" where you can step back, neutralize your emotions, and make better decisions.

Here are the steps of the Neutral tool:

1. Take a time-out, breathing slowly and deeply. Imagine the air entering and leaving through the heart area or the center of your chest.

2. Try to disengage from your stressful thoughts and feelings as you continue to breathe.

3. Continue until you have neutralized the emotional charge.

After you use *Awareness and BEing Gentle*, and admit what you are feeling, if you were unable to ease the stress out, use *BEing Neutral* to help align your heart, mind and emotions to neutralize the stressful feeling. You take a time-out by choosing to step back from the stress feeling and release the emotional significance you are placing on the issue. Step 1 helps draw the energy out of your head, where negative thoughts and feelings get amplified. Just breathe slowly and deeply in a casual way as you imagine the air entering and leaving through the center of your chest and heart area. In Step 2, just having the intent to disengage from stressful thoughts and feelings, as you continue to breathe through the heart, can help you release a lot of the emotional energy. In Step 3, you continue the process until you have chilled out and neutralized the emotional charge.

Using *BEing Neutral* doesn't mean that your frustration, worry or other stressful feeling will have totally evaporated. It just means that the charged energy has been taken out and you have stopped the stress accumulation. Even if you can't totally neutralize the stressful feeling, just the effort to shift into neutral will give you a chance to regroup your energies and refocus. As you practice *BEing Neutral* you will build your power to tell intrusive disturbing thoughts and feelings, "Thanks for stopping by, but I'm not going to feed you," and mean it. This will start to change your emotional diet—the feelings and thoughts you keep feeding yourself. You will begin to see more clearly what triggers your emotional habits and you'll build power to neutralize the emotional drive fueling your habit.

Practicing *BEing Neutral* helps you to "rewire" and balance your nervous system and hormones, which makes it easier to neutralize emotional stress. You start to feel better about yourself, and a positive feedback loop is created whereby emotional management reinforces a physiological change, and the physiological change makes it easier to neutralize stress. Each time you go to *Neutral*, you are taking an important step to reprogram both your emotional and physical habit patterns. It helps to remember that it won't always be as difficult to go to *Neutral* as it can seem in the beginning; as you establish new neural habits, it gets easier and easier!

TOOL #3—THE QUICK COHERENCE TECHNIQUE

Heart Focus: Focus your attention in the area of your heart, in the center of your chest.

If your mind wanders, just keep shifting your attention back to the heart while you do Steps 2 and 3.

Heart Breathing: As you focus on the area of your heart, imagine your breath is flowing in and out through that area.

This step helps your mind and energy to stay focused in the heart area and your respiration and heart rhythms to synchronize. Breathe slowly and gently in through your heart and out through your heart (as if your mouth were in your heart). Do this until your breathing feels smooth and balanced, not forced. Continue to breathe with ease until you find a natural inner rhythm that feels good to you.

Heart Feeling: As you continue to breathe through the area of your heart, recall a positive feeling, a time when you felt good inside, and try to re-experience it. Once you've found it, try to sustain the positive feeling by continuing Heart Focus, Heart Breathing, and Heart Feeling.

Heart feeling could be a feeling of appreciation or care toward a special person or a pet, a place you enjoyed, or an activity that was fun. Allow yourself to feel this good feeling of appreciation or care. If you can't feel anything, it's okay; just breathe the attitude of appreciation or care.

Step 3: Changing Your Emotional Diet

The third step in this Program is to identify your emotional habits, and learn how you can change your emotional diet.

1. Take the drama and significance out of emotional reactions.
2. Refocus your emotional energy and shift your emotional state to align with your core heart values.
3. Connect with your heart intelligence and intuitive discernment.

Not living up to our own expectations can become an obsession that consumes a lot of our thoughts, feelings and energy. Then the emotional diet we are feeding ourselves is full of self-judgment, self-blame, guilt, despair and shame, all of which drain our energy and make us want to comfort ourselves with chocolate or alcohol or something that will distract us from our true goal.

It's important that we acknowledge, neutralize and release the negative emotions and attitudes that we feed ourselves. It's equally important that we learn how to refocus our emotional energy and shift our emotional state to comfort ourselves from inside-out. Using the list of other activities and behaviors that bring comfort as replacements for seeking comfort in your addiction can also help to activate positive feelings from your own heart first.

1. Take a time-out so that you can temporarily disengage from your thoughts and feelings—especially stressful ones.
2. Shift your focus to the area around your heart. Now, feel your breath coming in through your heart and

out through your heart. *Practice this for ten seconds or longer.*

3. Make a sincere effort to activate a positive feeling. This can be a genuine feeling of appreciation or care for someone, some place or something in your life.

4. Ask yourself what would be an efficient, effective attitude or action that would balance and de-stress your system.

5. Quietly sense any shifts in perception, attitude or feelings. *Find a less stressful perspective and stay with the shift or the change as long as you can.*

QUICK START: TOOL CHEAT SHEET

Awareness and Being Gentle:

1. Notice and admit what you are feeling.

2. Try to name the feeling.

3. Tell yourself to e-a-s-e, as you gently focus in your heart, relax as you breathe and e-a-s-e the stressful feeling out.

Power of BEing Neutral:

1. Take a time-out, breathing slowly and deeply.

2. Imagine the air entering and leaving through the heart area or the center of your chest.

3. Try to disengage from your stressful thoughts or feelings as you continue to breathe through the heart area until you have neutralized the emotional charge.

Quick Coherence:

1. Heart Focus: Focus your attention in the area of your heart, in the center of your chest.

2. Heart Breathing: As you focus on the area of your heart, imagine your breath flowing in and out through that area.

3. Heart Feeling: As you continue to breathe through the area of your heart, recall a positive feeling, a time when you felt good inside, and try to re-experience it.

Attitude Breathing:

1. Admit the feeling or attitude that you want to change, such as anger, anxiety, blame, sadness, self-judgment, boredom, frustration, guilt, feeling over-whelmed, etc.

2. Breathe a replacement attitude (make a list). You do this by selecting a positive attitude and then breathing the feeling of that new attitude in slowly and casually through your heart area. For example, if you are worried, breathe calm. This requires breathing the attitude of calm until you actually feel more calmed. That's when you have made the energetic shift.

3. Keep breathing the feeling of the new attitude to make it more real.

A Heart's Way is the 2nd Part of Power of the Heart: How to Align to your Soul's Purpose and Manifest your True Dreams

1. Get clear about what you really desire.

Many of us have mastered our minds and spent inordinate skill and time to build this capacity. However, our mind and ego live from our past experiences, our emotional attachments and our reactions. We believe that our hearts require protection from the experiences that have hurt us in the past. Yet, it is our hearts that have the power to free us from this pain and struggle. Our hearts hold the space of our soul's purpose. When you can uncover all the beliefs, fears, thoughts, expectations, anxieties, etc., that protect your heart, you will create space for your heart's and soul's full expression.

In these times of uncertainty and confusion, we are often unclear about what we want. We are, on the other hand, usually very clear about what we don't want—the abusive or emotionally unavailable partner, the unfulfilling career or our looming debt, all the fears and beliefs that keep us focused outside of ourselves, a world that has created victims and submissive people who have learned to repress our dreams, because we were disappointed or we were discouraged to hold onto our dreams. *The problem with this is that whatever we focus on, we attract more of into our lives.* However, in order to find our path to our heart so we can align with our soul's purpose and hear its gentle guidance, we need to set clearer intentions and know what we want in our lives.

MAIN AREAS OF FOCUS

Relationships are an area where we often think about all the problems within current relationships or in past ones, hoping that we will not recreate our mistakes. However, as we focus on that abusive relationship or emotionally unavailable partner, we tend to continue our patterns instead of creating the healthy relationship we desire.

Health areas are very challenging because, often, it isn't until there is a problem that we realize how much energy we have been spending worrying about something, which could often be unrelated to illness. It is the *stress* of this worry, however, that creates dis-ease. Then, once we have a diagnosis, physical pain or excess weight, the ability to focus on a healthy body is even more challenging.

Career issues are most often with the relationships within our work environment. While these days, we are all being asked to consider what truly makes us happy and our hearts sing, instead, much of our attention is focused on the conflicts between co-workers and the silly gossip that takes place in our work environments. With all of that, we barely have time to consider our passions.

Money issues have been in the center of our minds for several years, as the collective unconscious has been reacting to this financial crisis that doesn't appear to be quickly getting better. We look at our debt and our bills and we worry about them each month. Survival issues make it extraordinarily difficult to focus on freedom and prosperity.

What I often suggest when determining what it is that you truly want, is to go back into your life and make a list of all the things you don't want, as this is often where we spend most of our focused time anyway. Look at these areas in your life and create a list of all the things you don't want. From that list, decide what you do want. Look at the beliefs, fears, thoughts, expectations and anxieties that you continue to hold in these areas. From this list, honestly contemplate what it is you desire.

However, be conscious of what it is you "believe" you truly want. Many people believe they desire money or winning the lottery, but this isn't what you actually want. Yes, it may relieve you of certain difficult situations, but ultimately, what we long for is *inner happiness*. In fact, if you explore all of your passions, you will uncover that happiness is what you actually want. There is a clue for you here as well; happiness comes from within you, not outside of you! So, what we actually yearn for are emotions that exist within us, not outside of us. Neither money nor external "things" can ever make us happy (for very long).

Since you have already learned some ways to work on your emotions, this will give you some clues to creating emotions that are positive in your life (the true things that your heart desires) although building your career, being in service, working on your emotional attachments and reactions, developing our spiritual growth and living your true purpose are worthy goals and our heart passion! In fact, it is very important to evolve our ego so that we aren't stuck in the lower emotions that keep us stuck. The tools from the first section allow us to become aware and let go of the emotions that prohibit us from living our dreams.

2. Uncover how limiting beliefs/habits/stories hold you back and keep you stuck.

What limiting beliefs, habits and stories do you have? Our stories center on our relationships with family, friends, partners, co-workers and/or bosses. We hold certain stuck emotions from our childhood that limit us from creating the life we desire, and keep us in our "head," choosing fear over our hearts and love. Our family and friends are where our earliest patterns develop, and they create the beliefs, habits and stories that shape the ways we live our lives. For example, my "story" has to do with abandonment, and my relationships and other situations in my life seem to reflect different aspects of this story. Our stories impact all of our relationships. They even affect situations that appear, on the outside, to be unrelated. These "unrelated" situations, however, elicit the same emotions we experienced as children. An example of this is you are having difficulty paying the bills, and because of this, you feel unsupported and abandoned. Not the same way as a child who has been abandoned, but the theme of abandonment runs through the situation and impacts how we react to the event.

We talk about changing our stories, yet, what are these stories? They are what we tell ourselves when something happens that we feel is personal—like I'm stupid, I'm always abandoned, I'm sad, unhappy, and lonely . . . you get the idea (story). Our initial reaction is authentic. We may feel frustrated, angry, excited, anxious, or a variety of emotions that are valid. However, it is after our initial response that we have the choice to choose how to respond next. This is the time when a story is either validated or created from our past experiences. As many ancient wisdom teachings suggest, all events are neutral; it is our choice to come from a conscious choosing of our response or adding to our story and letting our unconscious reaction hold us prisoner.

It is our *choices* that determine whether we are evolving or not. When we become so invested in the game and what we perceive as our "story," that we use to justify our fear and our ego, we begin to identify ourselves as the game or story. We forget who we really are. We get so caught up in our story that we put all of our energy on fixing, manipulating, or trying to control the game in our search for happiness that we may miss the very reason we are here at this time, in this human experience. We are here to evolve! *Evolution occurs when we make choices from a state of being that is love, not fear.* All the stories we create around justifying our choices that are not love, move us away from our soul's goal, which is our free will to make choices that allow us to evolve our consciousness or not!

Knowing that our initial reaction is unconscious and valid, we then have the opportunity to evolve our consciousness by choosing to rewrite our story—seeing the event as neutral and allowing ourselves the opportunity to view what happens as just something that happens, and it is NOT personal to us. It isn't about what someone else has done to us or that they are trying to hurt us; it is just an event. We can now choose to accept our initial reaction and be gentle to ourselves by knowing that it is perfectly authentic to express emotions. Every emotion is necessary and has a natural movement of energy that is beneficial to us. Anger expressed authentically can get us moving towards a powerful action, especially if we are in a depressed state.

However, if it builds upon our "story" of *I'm angry because this always happens to me,* and we give the anger a story to hold onto, then we get stuck in the story of what happened to us. Yet, we always have another opportunity to make another choice.

It is important still to be authentic and allow our emotions to be felt; however, once we have our initial reaction in the now moment, we must be vigilant to not add to the story of why we felt our initial reaction. Just ask yourself, how can I come from a state of love now? By allowing the opportunity to feel and express our initial emotion of anger and then examine what happened, we can then make a choice to grow our consciousness and change our neural pathways and create new ones.

It takes time to learn to catch ourselves in the act of creating a story around a situation. Once the story is there, we need to fully see our story, where it came from, and begin to let it go. Letting go is easier said than done, but it is essential to allowing us to come from a state of love. After you have mastered and embraced making a choice from a state of love, we still have more to let go of! We must then let go of all expectations and any need to see the "outcome" of our loving choice.

We need to really want to make our choices from a state of love instead of fear, because that is how we evolve our consciousness, not because it will make our "outside" world better. Our outside world is just part of the game. How much money or accumulation of conveniences *is not* the focus. Our focus is on evolving our consciousness towards love. We have to let go of the desire to manipulate the game or have the game meet our timing preferences. We also need to let go of the "happenings" within the game and just focus on our choices. Then our stories become forever changed and our old story lines can no longer imprison us.

3. Live in Present Moment Awareness. Break through your patterns and reactions to be in charge of your responses.

During these interesting times, I find it increasingly important to be "present." Practicing mindfulness and being in the moment is always a great morning exercise to ensure you are ready to set your intentions for the day. Eckhart Tolle suggests that you practice being present by becoming aware of your body and its responses or feelings. This means you can't be in the "past" or worrying about the future.

To live in the present moment requires us to be focused on the here and now, instead of worrying about the future or regretting the past. When you aren't living in the now, you are most likely living in the past, by looking at a person from your past event that you wish you had done differently or remembering something you want to hold onto. Or, you are in the future, projecting your hopes or your fears. Many of us spend a majority of our lives either reflecting on the past or projecting into the future. We need to learn to break through our patterns and reactions, so that we can be in charge of our responses. We would all like to be in *control* of our lives. However, there are always situations, events and people who can interfere with our sense of *being*. Usually, someone or something triggers us, and we unconsciously react to what we feel has *happened* to us. We may feel amazing one moment and be triggered into a reaction the next. Sometimes it is our own ego that triggers our unconscious reaction, by bringing up a past memory or a future worry.

Clearly, we are not in control over our sense of *being*, let alone our ego/mind. However, we can be in charge of our responses when we identify our patterns and know our reactions. When we can identify how our body reacts to situations and people, then we can begin to shift our focus to be in charge of our responses. In the beginning, it may be after we have already reacted and are in our pattern. However, the more aware you are, the more opportunity you have to begin to shift and come into the present moment, so that you can be conscious and in charge of your response.

What does it mean to be in charge of your response? It means that you have a choice on how you respond to any given situation or person. Only *you* can choose how you want to respond emotionally. You have a choice: you can choose to respond from a place of peace, from present moment awareness, or from a place of unconscious reaction.

To be grounded, first you must be present in your mind and body, and from that place of inner balance, connect in with the earth. Often we think of connecting with the Divine and forget to connect with the earth. However, the earth is where we reside, and grounding into the earth and connecting with the Divine Mother is crucial for our manifestation and creation process. The earth offers the best outlet to send the energies you need cleared. Our Divine Mother is the nurturer, not only of this planet, but she can and will nurture and heal us when we invite her in our hearts.

Which brings me to balance—I believe that the last exercise we require in the morning before we rise is to balance ourselves. "Balance" has different definitions to many people. We can balance our chakras (energy centers), meridians or our body's magnetics. Recently I bought an EMF device that balances Wi-Fi, cell phone, electromagnetic radiation, and geopathic stress within my home, and it has allowed me to feel very balanced. Whatever method or technique you use, grounding has the ability to have a significant impact on your health and well-being. When these exercises are all done in sequence, it offers you the best option for setting your intentions for the day.

Being in a state of balance is about more than our energy; it is about finding a way to harmonize all areas of our lives. It is like the 7 of Cups in the Tarot, which represents, to me, how we can find balance in all the areas of our lives that we have dreams in. Often we desire a relationship but forget to visualize or understand how a relationship fits into all the areas of our life. Relationships play a much more important function in our lives as women than they do for men. However, this relationship we seek may not fit into our career as a whole, and it may take sacrifice to maintain the relationship we seek.

So, it is very important when wanting to create something, to find balance within all areas of our lives.

Grounding ourselves and finding balance within the chaos that exists on this planet, and perhaps in our lives, is key to living a mindful life. We often are taken off balance when events occur in our lives or when events occur to our planet. If we begin with becoming present, then grounding and balancing ourselves, it can open us to finding a way to be in harmony with all areas of our lives. When we integrate living from this place of harmony, we become more aware of when we are unbalanced and can stabilize ourselves before we get caught up in the chaos. Living in this way enables us to take on the responsibility of our own growth, well-being and our spiritual evolution.

The easiest way to live in present moment awareness is to practice conscious breathing. When you feel stressed, road rage, or anxious, focus on your breathing. You can also focus on your body, how you're feeling, where you are, and what you're doing. Try walking barefoot on the earth, stretching your energy deep into the soil like a tree, or really connect and breathe into all that living in the present offers you.

4. Shift from your head to your heart with the tools that lead to acceptance, non-judgment and witness consciousness. Find practices that still the mind, body, and spirit so you can hear the gentle guidance of the heart.

I would like to invite you to begin to shift from your head to your heart. We are predominantly in our heads most of the time, reflecting the past, and projecting into the future. We distract ourselves with an array of *doings*, from trying to understand ourselves better, to trying to change ourselves, to trying to fix or heal ourselves. However, through this we are still trying to *do* something, which means we are in our heads. I want to encourage you to experience another way—moving from your heads and forever doing something, to dropping into your hearts where you can *be*! Moving from our heads to our bodies, and ultimately our heart, means we are not *doing* but *BEing*. We can then respond to situations and people by *BEing* loving (for ourselves or others) instead of reacting unconsciously from fear because we are in our heads and not in the present moment.

The first part of this process is to learn acceptance. Instead of trying to *Do* something, we can learn to *Be*, which means that we learn to accept our circumstances instead of resisting them. Accept ourselves for who we are, and let that inner being shine through. The wounded aspect of ourselves has been misguided through our unconscious belief system. Feeling into our heart allows us to accept all areas of our lives, and to embrace the difficult along with the uniqueness that is YOU. This requires a surrender into your heart, knowing that you are divinely perfect.

Since we love conditionally, we seem to make judgments on everything. Our minds are always in competition to be loved. Therefore, we judge whether someone is superior or inferior to us. We judge those areas we want to be accepted within ourselves. We need to discover a way to accept everyone, including ourselves, without expectations and judgment. This is only something you can do when you are present and in the flow of being, in your heart. Our heads don't know how to live without making a judgment.

Lastly, we need to come from a place of witness consciousness, which means being fully present in the here and now. When we are in our heads, we cannot be present. In our heads we are reliving the past or worrying about the future. Our bodies, and ultimately our hearts, are where we can observe life, end judgments and embrace acceptance of our lives. We are perfect and imperfect, because we are human and creating our conscious being. From shifting from our heads to our hearts we can find the way to hear the gentle guidance of our soul.

5. Trusting your Intuition and your Innate Inner Guidance. Begin to Express your Authenticity, the natural soul essence of who you are.

LISTENING TO OUR INTUITION

When we focus on our heart, we find the still space, the quiet connection where we can hear our gentle guidance from our hearts. Our hearts will guide us through the stillness where our souls express who we are. Intuition is a skill that is built through practice and through finding that stillness where we can truly listen. Our hearts hold the divine spark of our souls. Finding that stillness within your heart brings you the purpose you are here to manifest. Expressing your soul's purpose will align you with infinite possibilities to manifest your dreams.

As a child (if you can look deep enough in your heart to remember this) what we all seek is to be loved and accepted for who we are. Unfortunately, many of us were convinced that who we were, was not good enough. As a result, from our childhood forward, we have not been authentic. We try to be someone we think everyone else will love. Authenticity is the freedom to remember who we are, by loving ourselves and accepting ourselves as we are. When you can uncover this love within you, you won't be bound by what others think and feel, and you can express who you have always been. We need to learn to *express our authenticity, the natural soul essence* that is us.

Being authentic in all relationships is the key. It must begin with ourselves and then move outward. It is primarily about the choices we make, because most of the time we are reacting from fear. How we were taught to love is often a result of manipulation and control. Most of our relationships center around love that has conditions, by fulfilling our wants and desires. For example, I will love you as long as you fit my fantasy "relationship." Mark Borax talks about radical intimacy, where we trust our partners enough to grant us the power to show us what we are not ready to see about ourselves. Relationships have the ability to show us our shadows, and we can then choose to accept them as part of who we are. This allows us an opportunity to respond from a place of love, which can transform our shadows and allow us to be loved and accepted for who we are, not who we think we should be.

Unconditional love is what we all seek. Instead, we hide our true selves and try to be someone else. Then we feel we are unheard, unseen, we build resentments and slowly shut down. We keep ourselves distracted through our addictions, reflecting on our pain from the past and projecting our fears in the future. When we are in the present, we can be more authentic; this honors our Self and allows for healing to begin.

Self-love means to become very conscious of all the "personalities" we have chosen. It is also about learning to choose to respond to situations from your authentic self, instead of unconsciously reacting from fear and our outdated behaviors. Relationships are where we learn the most about who we are, whether they are friends, family, co-workers, or romantic relationships. When we choose to be authentic, we choose to love and accept ourselves for who we are. This allows our soul essence to shine, and allows us to fully live our lives, while keeping our hearts open.

PRACTICES FOR RECEIVING THE GENTLE GUIDANCE OF THE SOUL

When it comes to receiving guidance, especially the gentle guidance of our soul, we all are quite unique. I have expanded my understanding of how our intuition works and, therefore, our ability to receive information from soul.

There are the four senses that we have always understood: clairvoyant, clairaudient, clairsentient (feeling) and claircognizant (knowing); however, I believe we also can expand these senses through our mental, emotional, physical and spiritual ways of experiencing our information.

How well we understand ourselves and how we learn, will assist us in understanding how we receive information and guidance. When we were young, the school system primarily used visual and auditory methods to teach us. For those of us who are empathic or download and just "know" information, this system failed us. I encountered and interviewed an author, Sherrie Dillard, who expands into how we receive information through our subtle bodies. To me, this suggests, we are expanding both clairsentience and claircognizance, as this has become much more prevalent in the past twenty plus years. My belief is that more and more people are clairsentient and claircognizant. This has allowed for us to move from our "third eye" to our hearts, where we are becoming more "heart centered."

So, understanding first how soul speaks to you will be important to how you receive information. I have found soul to express itself very gently, through nudges of passion, joy and excitement. For me, these emotions indicate that inner urge to explore the source of this passion, joy and excitement. I typically have to be quiet and go within—finding that space that allows me to feel at "home." If I am reacting from fear, or am stressed, out of sorts, or confused, I will miss the gentle nudges of the soul.

We all have different ways we can receive this information. Some people meditate by walking, or connecting with nature. Others require many senses to be occupied; i.e., with incense, music, bath, candles, warm tea. Finding your preferred method will assist you to receive soul's messages.

Emotional people experience life with their hearts wide open. *Mental* people don't use their mind as much as they receive a higher guidance from consciousness. *Physical* people feel through their bodies. *Spiritual* people experience an energetic vibration. Engaging any of these primary energetic bodies will allow you to experience soul more effectively. So, we take the clairsentient person, who feels, but may feel through mental guidance, receiving symbols that have a certain feeling to them.

Once you understand yourself and can identify your primary ways of receiving guidance, you then have to practice. Through practice comes trust.

6. Align with your soul purpose, where you can feel more confident, empowered, and live from inner happiness to manifest your true dreams.

Your soul's purpose is being radiated from you every moment of the day. Aligning with this and being able to uncover the gentle guidance of your soul is the goal of our work together.

We all have core values and purpose that resonate with our core being. Once you align with your purpose, you will feel more confident and empowered. This will also bring clarity to manifesting your true dreams.

I have struggled with creating our reality, especially with Law of Attraction (LOA), because there are many different laws of this universe, and relying on just one of them to create everything in your life doesn't feel right to me. Consider the following:

1. What is your motivation to create something? It isn't necessarily as simple as choosing fear versus love. Rather, it is often something we are trying to "change, fix, heal, manipulate or control" from a place of fear. We need to ask ourselves, what do we want to accomplish with this goal, change, etc.? If we keep asking the question "why?" the answer will almost always be happiness in some form or another. Our motivation to change, have a million dollars, a better relationship, a better career, etc., is all about the pursuit for *inner happiness*.

2. What is "happiness?" What does it even mean? It is most definitely an inner feeling/emotion. It definitely isn't *out* there. It is a frequency of energy that is labeled good. But, what is it? We seem to be on this outer search for something that can only be fulfilled from within ourselves. However, when we feel emptiness within our being or a void that is longing for something, we begin to create from this place of longing and emptiness in our outer world. When we try and fill this longing within our hearts and souls with outside *things* in hopes of creating a more fulfilling and happy life, it doesn't work. No matter how much we *do* the "right things," when we

attempt to mold our outer reality without connecting with and addressing our inner reality, we will not be successful.

3. We continue to watch our outside world for validation that we are *doing* it right and creating what we desire. However, it can never be created from the outside-in! So why is our focus on validating our outside world? We are not defined by our outer world, but from our inner world. When we continue to focus on what we can *do* to change, fix, heal, control and manipulate our outside world, then we are creating from a void in our inner world, not the other way around! It is almost as if we are trying to will our desired reality into being. Unfortunately, creating the life you love is not about a battle of wills. The sheer force of your desire will not manifest your hopes and dreams until you understand how to create in harmony with your inner self.

Currently we believe that if we want something different in our outside world, we need to do something different! LOA taught us that if we change our thoughts, our emotional responses (that are unconscious) and are *doing* it right, then our outer world will change. What I now understand is that we have to change our inner feelings to fill us up and then allow our inner world to create our outside experience. We have to stop marking our successes from what we see outside, since it isn't "real" anyway, but rather just a hologram of our inner world.

Repeatedly we are told to look outside for our validation! That is why so many spiritual teachers talk about non-attachment. That doesn't mean we have to give up our passion and excitement for our lives! When our energy is constantly searching the outside world to prove we are doing it "right" we continue to put our focus on our outside world. We can still create the world that our soul and imagination desire, but we create it from *within*!

If our state of being is compromised by a void of some kind, we are going to be creating from our fears, whether we are aware of it or not. However, if we commit to an inner journey that acknowledges that void or place of fear, then we can truly begin to create a beautiful life. That beautiful life will be a reflection of our beauty and our divinity, which we have allowed to blossom within us. See the world for the hologram that it is. If you want to change something in your life, first connect with your soul and your heart and fill up your inner world with who you truly are! It is all just a change in perspective!

The Realities of Creation offers you a variety of ways to create your new reality. I know that the power of the heart has the ability to shift you out of stress, into a coherent state so that you can use the electromagnetic field to manifest your dreams. I also know it is important to be aware of yourself and what you truly desire—what your motivation is and setting your intentions to create. You can discover your soul's purpose by understanding who you are and by getting connected to your inner being.

During my research and through many radio shows with a variety of different people and modalities, I have established that there are different beliefs on our purpose. David Watson, who channels his soul group, The Willows, believes our purpose is to have emotional experiences and to make choices. What does this mean? We are here to experience a variety of emotions, and to thrive in our life. We are here to dive into this experience called life. CARPE DIEM! *"The purpose of life is to live it, to taste experience to the utmost, to reach out eagerly and without fear for newer and richer experience." (Eleanor Roosevelt).* However, we are also to make choices on how we respond to these experiences. We often take things too personally, and when things happen, we interpret them as happening to us, which causes us to react from a place of fear. Rather, we need to come from a place of neutrality and decide how we would like to respond to each event in our lives. Make choices from a place of love rather than fear.

Another belief about purpose (this focus came from a 15-year-old crystal child in the book, *Conversations with the Children of Now* by Meg Blackburn Losey) is that we have a *minor purpose* and a *major purpose*, and both are of equal importance. Our minor purpose is to have fun. This would be similar to having emotional experiences, although, with the emphasis in remembering that this is a game—to enjoy the entire process, not get caught up in the heaviness we often get stuck and lost in. Stop taking life so seriously and actually have some FUN! When was the last time you had any fun?

The major purpose is to make a difference. This is where our soul purpose falls. However, we have many different opportunities to make a difference in this world. It is our choice on how we do this. Yes, there are some things that we are better at than others. We are also quite unique in who we are. However, it truly is our choice. This is what also correlates to The Willows' definition about making choices. Our parents may have influenced us on what career path we chose; however, if we dived in and excelled at it, it was our choice to do this. Others choose to forego their educated professions and dive into something else, sometimes even hobbies, but they still make a difference.

The second part of this belief about purpose is that we evolve them. To evolve our purpose, we need to understand how we make a difference, how our soul can make a difference; to acknowledge the light within ourselves; to utilize that light for the greater good, and then expand that by taking it to the next level of making a difference. We make a difference through the loving choices we make. We make a difference by allowing our soul to know and experience this choice. And we must have fun, and enJOY the entire process, through our variety of experiences. If either has not been achieved, we would feel like we failed once we left this plane of existence.

As we often struggle to figure out how to make a difference, maybe that is not where we need to be focusing right now, but rather on what is fun—contemplate how to have more fun in your life—delivering yourself into higher levels of fun, knowing what that feels like inside of you. Learn to dance in this gift called life.

So, to align with your soul's purpose is to connect with your heart, keep the heart clear and in a coherent state, and listen to your inner guidance—those gentle nudges that make you feel passionate about life. To *"Follow your Bliss" (Joseph Campbell),* choose to acknowledge what makes you happy. Uncover your inner happiness, not from how you react outside of yourself, but by choosing to be *happy* in all you do! It comes from doing or BEing in a state of love, instead of fear. So, know your motivation for everything you do. As you live with purpose, making a difference in *your* world (this will impact the world and universe) and enJOYing your life, you will feel more confident and empowered. And your soul will whisper and guide you to living your soul's purpose. This is the power of the heart!

DREAMS DURING THE AGE OF AQUARIUS: SIX BENEFITS FOR YOU

Kathleen O'Keefe-Kanavos

"All our dreams can come true, if we
have the courage to pursue them."
—Walt Disney

Did you know that you are still a dreamer in the Age of Aquarius? *Back to the Future* is moving forward with the convergence of religion, spirituality, and dreams. How does this shift impact your world and Universal Wisdom? The answer lies behind the veil of consciousness pulled back by guided dreams.

According to different astrologers' calculations, the Age of Aquarius is approximately 1447 AD to 3597 AD. The shift—shaking belief systems to their core—has escalated inner-guidance phenomena that defies logic, conventional measurement, and challenges some current religions, but is validated by life experiences. Some guided messages are simple, "Listen and live, or don't and die."

How attuned are you to this spiritual transition?

In popular culture in the United States, the Age of Aquarius refers to the advent of the New Age movement in the 1960s and 1970s. Astrologers, healers and dreamers take a different view. They see the Age of Aquarius as being a time in space that has been here for eons. An astrological age is a product of the earth's slow precessional rotation and lasts for 2,160 years, on average. That is 1 degree every 72 years. 360 / 12 zodiac signs = 30. 30 x 72 = 2,160. To a degree we are literally a part of the movement and only nearing the center point on that astrological time-continuum. Our generation will be permanent dreamers in the Age of Aquarius.

What does that mean for your health, healing, and dreams?

We will not see the end of the Age of Aquarius in this lifetime, but if you believe in reincarnation and play your cards right by respecting the finite qualities of the earth, you may be a part of the ending celebration in future lifetimes. In the meantime, we can still dream dreams that diagnose your life now.

Current-day prophetic guided dreams that came true

Dreams as an innate healing and diagnostic tool for a healthy daily life were first respected and used in the ancient societies of Egypt and Greece. Dreaming was considered a supernatural communication or means of divine intervention.

Ancient Greeks constructed temples called *asclepions*, where the sick were cured through divine grace by incubating dreams. This was a convergence of spirituality and religion. Dream encounters with angels or spirit guides were considered to be of particular significance.

Current books describe the dreaming brain but few, if any, discuss studies on intuitive/dream approaches to the acquisition of knowledge about disease—until now.

Current guided dream case studies

Extraordinary dreams that guide, heal and change lives are being collected and shared by dreamers and researchers worldwide. In 2013, a project was initiated on dreams that diagnosed breast cancer that is jointly sponsored by Healing Imager, Inc., and Dreams Book, Inc., with IRB (Institutional Review Board) approval by the Rhine Research Center. Larry Burk, MD, CEHP, is the principal investigator.

Dr. Larry Burk and his research patient Kathleen O'Keefe-Kanavos (me) whose prophetic lucid dreams diagnosed three cancers missed by the medical community and the tests on which they relied, have been working to bring dreams back into medicine. My book, *Surviving Cancerland: Intuitive Aspects of Healing* (Cypress House), attracted Dr. Burk's attention as it described in detail my precognitive dreams validated by pathology reports.

Dr. Burk and I presented these findings to doctors from around the world at the 2014 International Association for the Study of Dreams (IASD) in Berkeley, CA. The research spotlights twenty patients as case studies whose dreams diagnosed breast cancer and has been submitted for publication to the 2014 Sept/Oct issue of *Explore: The Journal of Science and Healing* -www.explorejournal.com/edboard.

Here is an extraordinary story by an ordinary person about the thinning veil between human consciousness and Divine guidance.

My yearly check-up had consisted of a mammogram, blood test and physical exam. My doctor told me that I was healthy and to go home. That night I had the first of many recurrent lucid precognitive guided dreams. A spirit guide dressed as a monk stepped through a pop-up window in my dream, much like a pop-up on a computer. This epic dream stopped as time stood still, a sign that this was a special dream containing important information.

The spirit guide took my hand, placed it on my breast and asked, "Do you feel that?" When I said yes, the guide replied, "That is breast cancer. Return to your doctor tomorrow," and the epic dream resumed as the guide disappeared through the pop-up dream window. The next day my doctor felt nothing but ordered another mammogram, again showing that I was healthy. When the spirit guide reappeared in my dream a third time, I began to cry and said, "My doctor won't listen to me." The guide handed me a white feather and said, "Return to your doctor tomorrow, and use this feather as a verbal sword to fence with his words, and you will get the exploratory surgery you need to find this cancer. You will win." Using the feather imagery, I returned to my doctor and convinced him to do surgery. Pathology reported a primary stage-two aggressive tumor in the right breast and a positive lymph node. Three years later, I was warned in a dream about three cancers in my lifetime by my physician-within named Dr. Jules.

Five years after that dream I was again warned of stage—four recurrence in a dream by spirit guides dressed as doctors who turned into scary circus clowns.

I understood that my nightmare was a frightening call-to-action. A double mastectomy revealed the third cancer—three crabs—all diagnosed by prophetic dreams. Guided dreams had saved my life.

Throughout this ordeal, my biggest challenge centered on whom to believe—doctors and their state-of-the-art tests that told me that I was healthy and to go home, or dream spirit guides dressed as Franciscan monks who told me that I had breast cancer. Who would not want to hear that they were healthy? What patient would not believe medical tests that "proved" a nightmare wrong? Yet, I chose my guided dreams over medical tests and lived to work with my doctors and thrive.

The deep well of guiding wisdom-universal consciousness

Dreams contain an ever-available deep well of guided wisdom. Dream guides take countless forms—angels, religious figures, earth mothers, black Madonnas, grandmothers, divine children, or mythological heroes. Any apparition that radiates numinous energy can communicate guidance.

Dream guides expand relationships in all aspects of life

Not all dreams contain life-altering information that must be remembered. However, when you are in crisis or plan to make the "mistake of a lifetime," your ET (Eternal Teacher) phones home for help. Dreams are phone lines to the *other side* answered by spirit guides.

On my live weekly Internet radio show, *Your Life and Purpose Revealed* (http://www.blogtalkradio.com/living-well-talk-radio), co-hosted with Suzanne Strisower, callers have shared warning dreams of financial ruin prompting them to pull money from the stock market before it crashed. Other callers speak of meeting their future husband in dreams or dreams that warned of pitfalls in their current relationship. Dreams are doorways to important guidance.

Dreamers bringing the guidance of dreams into waking life have reported these six benefits:

- Decreased feelings of anxiety and stress
- Increased sense of confidence in problem solving
- Improved relationships with both personal and inter-personal issues
- Increased feelings of hope
- Increased feelings of peace of mind and how to live fully, no matter the circumstances
- Increased sense of connection to inner guidance resources

Conclusion

Inner guidance is an innate gift. Popular musician Paul McCartney sings about how during times of trouble his deceased mother, Mary, comes to him, sharing words of wisdom. The list of celebrities, politicians, scientists, and doctors whose dreams made a difference in their world, and yours, is long. Albert Einstein's $E=MC^2$ is a dream come true, as was President Abraham Lincoln's precognitive nightmare of his own impending assassination. Unfortunately, President Lincoln did not fully understand the language or symbolism in the dream.

Lewis Carroll's book *Alice Through the Looking-Glass* is a dreamscape. Alice tries to find her way out of the woods but can't see the forest for the trees. The vocabulary of the "Jabberwocky" is dream-speak—a confusing language that doesn't make sense . . . until you learn it. By learning your dream language by journaling your dreams, you will begin to understand the important information they contain.

Information that has emerged through patients' dreams will transform and transcend both religious and scientific claims. We're going "back to the future" where, like the ancient Egyptians and Greeks, dreams will be used as a diagnostic tool for health and healing, and as a respected means of unconscious guidance for a more awakened life.

Dreams were diagnostic tools used by Ancient Greeks and Egyptians. The modern day medical community is starting to discover how important dreams and healing are with the research work of Dr. Larry Burk, and the validated stories of his study group patients.

This begs the question, "Is medicine traveling 'back to the future' to find itself during the Age of Aquarius?" Is this a sign that spirituality, religion, and medicine are realigning like the stars to become more powerful than ever before? Are the psyche and the physical finally mending the fragmented image of divided self by using dreams as glue? Validated current research is answering, "Yes!"

Diagnostic dreams are messages that do come true.

PERSPECTIVE

Linda Minnick

"We are all in the gutter, but some
of us are looking at the stars."
—Oscar Wilde, *Lady Windermere's Fan*

Per·spec·tive: the interrelation in which a
subject or its parts are mentally viewed

A few days after my father's funeral in 1980, my sisters and I
were beginning to sort through Dad's belongings. As you do
when you are with your siblings, our conversations tended to
be around growing up in the very house we were now beginning to clear out. During a conversation, my older sister was
making a point about something and attributed the situation
to the fact that we were so poor. To this my reaction was,
"Excuse me? What do you mean we were poor?"

She looked at me as if I had two heads (which really wasn't
an uncommon response from my siblings)! "What do you

mean, 'What do you mean?'" she said and proceeded to point out all of the facts and events that supported her statement.

Poor? It never occurred to me that we were poor. In fact, I was blown away. You see, I had a wonderful childhood. I had everything I needed or wanted. I always had plenty of food, clothing, toys, a family that loved me, and a great house. I never wanted for anything. I knew from television that we weren't rich, and I knew from the mission work done through church that there were a lot of people worse off than I was. So obviously, we weren't poor. I really thought we were just good old "middle class." This really, really bothered me that my sister had a totally different perspective on her/our childhood.

This "revelation" followed me back to my own home, and I couldn't get it out of my head. I tried to figure it out. She is nine years older than I am. Perhaps my parents' circumstances were different when she was little than when I was little. It got to a point where I really needed to figure out where this was coming from. After reviewing in my head over and over again, it became clear that the only real difference in our experiences had to do with high school. As I thought about it, things began to click.

With the exception of college, I went all the way through school in the same neighborhood. I went to school with the same kids I played with after school. All of us lived in the same blue- collar area. All of us came from homes of working-class parents. All of us were on even status. No one had any more or any less than anyone else. We all had the same type of clothes, the same type of toys and bikes. We spent all our summer together at the city park. We pretty much lived very similar lives.

My sister, however, had earned a full scholarship to a very expensive private all-girls' high school. This meant that for the four years of high school instead of walking to school, she was bussed from our neighborhood to a more elite area of town, an area of town where the majority of people could afford to send their daughters to a private school. So instead of being surrounded by a student body of equal peers, she spent her days in the company of girls who did not have to wear homemade uniforms, who didn't have to bring bag lunches, who were able to take vacations during the summer, who had no problem saying "yes" to any of the extracurricular activities that required additional means to participate. While educationally she was on a much higher plane, I spent my high school years in a world of "yes," but she spent her high school years in a world of "no."

Bottom line is that even though we grew up with the same parents, in the same house, eating the same food, we had totally different experiences and formed totally different perceptions around our lives.

"Facts matter not at all. Perception is everything. It's certainty."
—Stephen Colbert

This really opened my eyes in regards to perception. I had always assumed that due to similarities in background, everyone in my life had—more or less—the same opinions and beliefs that I had. It wasn't long after this event that I began to recognize that there was more to creating an individual's belief system than I understood. This began my quest for more information about the process of thought—conscious and subconscious.

While some humans have been looking for answers regarding our brain, beliefs and perceptions since the dawn of creation, it was not a common table topic in 1980. Fast forward to the 21st century, and you can't walk past a magazine stand without some article about the brain and the way it works. It turns out, that like me, most of us are hungry to understand why we think the way we think and why we believe what we believe.

Science is now giving us concrete information about the differences between our conscious and subconscious minds and how they work. We are beginning to understand the consequences that our thoughts have on our lives. And, as if repeating the scene from the 1976 movie, *Network*, many of us are standing up and screaming, "We're mad as hell and we're not going to take this anymore!"

So if you are on this road of trying to understand how your perspective affects your life and how can you change it, let's give you a brief overview of the process.

The birth of perspective

It starts at conception. From conception to about six or seven, our subconscious mind absorbs everything that goes on around us, everything that is said, and everything that it witnesses. It has no choice. It doesn't have a filter or the ability to judge as to whether or not to keep the information. It takes the information, stores it and then uses it to create our "operating program"—otherwise known as the subconscious. As we continue to grow, anything else that leaves an impression—good or bad—is then added to the "programming" and soon this programming becomes your view of the world— your perspective—your belief system.

Based on the Szegedy-Maszák study of 2005, it has been determined that the subconscious mind shapes 95 percent or more of our life experiences. In the *Biology of Belief*, Dr. Bruce Lipton writes:

". . . Since subconscious programs operate without the necessity of observation or control by the conscious mind, we are completely unaware that our subconscious minds are making our everyday decisions. Our lives are essentially a printout of our subconscious programs, behaviors that were fundamentally acquired from others (our parents, family and community) before we were six years old. As psychologists recognize, a majority of these developmental programs are limiting and disempowering. . ."

If we pay attention, we can see this in our everyday lives. Have you ever been behind the wheel of a car in deep thought and made it to wherever you were going without realizing how you got there? It's programmed in your subconscious. Or if you have children, have you ever automatically responded to them with a comment or retort that came straight out of your mom or dad's mouth? (Usually something you swore you would never say!) Again, it's programmed in your subconscious.

Jane: Jane was one of four members of a vision workshop that I was holding. It was a 12-week program and during that time, Jane did everything that was asked of her. She wrote her vision. She listened to the tapes. She did the work in the workbook. She read and re-read her vision. She wrote affirmations.

She did *everything*. After several weeks, Jane was seeing positive changes in a few areas of her life such as her working conditions. But anything that had to do with finances was at a standstill. I recognized that there was something much deeper going on with Jane than what appeared on the surface. After a few one-on-one consultations with her, it became obvious to both of us. Jane had a subconscious belief in the lack of money. In order to create more abundance in her life, she had to create a new belief.

The importance of understanding our perceptions

Let's go back to Dr. Lipton. *". . . When it comes to sheer neurological processing abilities, the subconscious mind is more than a million times more powerful than the conscious mind. If the desires of the conscious mind conflict with the programs in the subconscious mind, which 'mind' do you think will win out? . . ."*

Knowing how our subconscious is formed and the power it contains gives us a better understanding of what it will take to make any kind of change in our life. Whether we are looking for more money, a better relationship, improved health, or a deeper spiritual connection, it helps to understand which "brain" we need to deal with. If the change we would like to make is in alignment with our programming, it may be a minor tweak to a subconscious thought. If it's something that is against what has been programmed, there is more work to be done. Most of our big changes come from this scenario (or they wouldn't be big changes)!

If we have been programmed to believe we are lacking in any way—not smart enough, not talented enough, the wrong (anything), not enough money, etc.—and we are trying to create a new lifestyle that goes against this belief, it's not going to help doing positive affirmations everyday if you can't get to the core belief. Once you get to the core belief and change it, you're ready to move forward.

"The new limitations are the human ones of perception."
—Milton Babbitt

Changing a belief

The bottom line to changing a belief or perception is finding the old thought and changing it. There are dozens of ways available to do this. Some are more successful than others. Some are as successful as the participant's faith in the process. We will discuss two.

The process I was using when working with Jane was thought control. In one way or another, thought control has been used for hundreds of years. This is a highly effective process especially for those who understand and believe that thoughts can be changed.

Thought control

The process I teach in my coaching has the person identify the new change they would like to see in their life. Once identified, they utilize a series of exercises to consistently focus on this change happening in their life.

It requires the brain to form a new thought pattern regarding the topic. To do this, they constantly and consciously send the brain message regarding the new topic. An example of the tools used in this process are:

- *Scripting*—Writing and re-writing a positive statement in present tense and first person. This action employs several of the senses and the repetition helps form that new neuro-pathway.

- *Vision board*—Pictures representing the changes. Again, employing multiple senses—visual and emotion.

- *Conscious thought control*—Consciously replacing any negative thoughts with positive. (Moving out of that "automatic" mode)

- *Visualization*—Quietly visualizing the change they want to create and, recognizing the change in vibration from where they currently are to the vibration of the new thought, stepping into that vibration and "putting on" the vision.

- *Use of media*—Positive audio, visual and reading material to re-enforce the power of the human spirit.

Needless to say, this process uses the repetition of these actions to create a new habit of thinking. It engages several different senses at the same time to add as much input as possible to assist in moving this process forward. As the name of the process says, it is thought control. This does take time. Typically the more deeply rooted the limiting belief, the longer the process.

This process, however, was not working for Jane. It was then that I realized that I needed an additional tool to help my clients. As I said before, there are dozens of different techniques. I looked at hypnosis, tapping (EFT {Emotional Freedom Technique}) and others. The process that I was attracted to and now utilize is *PSYCH-K®*.

PSYCH-K®

I was attracted to this process for several reasons. It's simple, direct, verifiable and, best of all, fast. (As a Virgo, I like things done quickly!) It utilizes the mind/body interface of muscle testing (kinesiology) to access the limiting thought. Through the use of left brain/right brain integration techniques, it produces swift and long-lasting changes. All of the work is permission-based through the access of the subconscious and the Higher Consciousness. Through this permission process, we work only on what is allowed and good for the client.

> *Jane*: Jane was one of my first clients for this process. In our hour together we worked on several areas around money. As this was not something where she could see an immediate result, she was not sure exactly how successful the session was. A week later I received a call from Jane. She had received an unexpected promotion within the company. With the new position, came additional money.

Unlike the thought control or other processes that take repeated sessions, PSYCH-K® produces immediate results.

> *Kate*: My daughter, Kate, joined us for a weekend family reunion. Kate was a senior in college and facing her mid-term calculus test. While she always did very well in other classes, since middle school, math was not her strong point. Kate had a middle school teacher who just berated her on several occasions in front of the class. From that point on, math was always her weakest subject. Her grades were

not where they needed to be to pass the class. We had only fifteen minutes of personal time. I facilitated a PSYCH-K® session for Kate around this subject. She returned to class that week and took her test. She received an A on the mid-term and pulled the overall class grade to a B.

One of the other benefits of PSYCH-K® is that, much like some other processes, it can be done in person or remotely.

Third part of the equation—Higher Consciousness

We have discussed how our perspective is formed and changed through our conscious and subconscious mind. We have yet to discuss how our Higher Consciousness works with our perception.

One of the questions I've always wanted an answer to is: "As a being of Higher Consciousness living in a brilliantly designed body, why do we have to deal with a subconscious that guides our lives with limiting thoughts?" While I don't have the entire answer, I do know that without our Higher Consciousness, I don't know how many of us would move forward into a better life.

I know for a fact that our Higher Consciousness "nudges" us when we need to move forward to our better selves. In doing so, I recognize that it has us questioning our belief systems and perceptions. It has us asking, "Why?" and "Why Not?" which then takes us to "How?"

It also plays a major part when we are working on the changes. It helps guide us, through intuition and other methods, to know what is right and what is wrong.

I would venture to guess that it is our Higher Consciousness that starts us on our paths to recognizing there is something better for us, that our lives are not complete. That we are living in a spiral universe that requires us to continue to grow and expand in our awesomeness!

The sum of the equation—you!

Our perception is our reality. There is no doubt about it. Only you can see your world as you see it. Only you can create your world as you want it. Now that we understand that, we can choose to believe our programming or we can choose to change it. Only you can decide what is right for you. It's your choice. It's your life. Know you are supported, loved and a vital part of this human family.

> *"What I had to learn was that I'm only*
> *responsible for my perception of things.*
> *The world's not out to get you.*
> *That's not the way it works."*
> —Chris Robinson

HOW TO GET A HIGHER SELF-CONNECTION

Maureen J. St. Germain

"When we pay attention, whatever we are doing . . . is
transformed and becomes part of our spiritual path."
—Rick Fields

How to achieve a Higher Self-Connection

In this chapter you will:

- Learn what the Higher Self is and is not and how to
  tell the difference
- Learn the first steps of talking and listening to your
  Higher Self
- Learn your Higher Self-connection is real, work with
  it fearlessly and with confidence
- Develop confidence with practice techniques that will
  assist with accurate Higher Self-connection
- Learn that there is only one question to ever ask your
  Higher Self.

What is the Higher Self?

The Higher Self is a version of *you* that is fully connected to God. Imagine for a moment that your Higher Self is like a circuit board that has unlimited potential. With your third dimensional expression, you have a very limited circuit board. If you put too much voltage through the circuit—you can burn it out. You can try to go directly to God, but because of your circuit board's limitation, your connection to God is restricted by who you are in the physical body, your beliefs, desires and experiences. You can expand your heart to increase your capacity. As you gain experience through the many practices offered in this book, you will discover that your capacity to know and express your love of God increases dramatically, along with your Higher Self-connection.

What's the Higher Self got—that I don't have?

The Higher Self is already fully connected to God. Your Higher Self is that part of YOU that is fully aware of himself (or herself) as you and as God. Some call the Higher Self the mediator, but even that implies separateness, which really isn't real. Your first goal is to communicate with your Higher Self. The next goal is to move your Higher Self presence into your physical body. Then you will be the walking ascended being! There is more after this.

What is the Higher-Self-connection?

The Higher Self-connection is something you build with a specific practice, that if done with diligence will provide you with highly accurate information in any time of need. Ultimately this is the first step in ascension work. The goal of ascension is to bring more of your God-self into physical form. When you do this, you are claiming your roots. You are claiming your heritage and can then step into the Divine being that you already are.

Imagine that you know someone who has direct Internet access. Every time you are on their computer, you have direct access. That direct access is easy and fast. You could use a dial- up connection, but once you have direct access (i.e., your Higher Self) you wouldn't want to go back to dial-up, and you don't have to.

The purpose of this section is to help you identify your Higher Self, work with developing your communication, and learn to get direct access to God through your Higher Self.

If it's me, why don't I already have it?
When you were born, you deliberately placed a` barrier between you in your physical body and who you really are in order to move your consciousness into physical matter. Once there, it is very likely that you will forget who you really are. The goal then is to re-connect you to yourself and become an enlightened being. You are not likely to do this instantly. You are moving through it slowly. You will maintain your aware-ness in the physical form, while bringing in more of your Divine Self. If you brought in all of your divinity at once, you would not be able to maintain your presence in your body; you would pop out of the physical dimension!

In your case, as you become more adapted and aware, allowing for integration of more and more of your Higher Self, then becoming the Higher Self is easily accomplished while maintaining your presence in the physical.

Once you have developed your Higher Self-connection to this new level, your Higher Self will communicate to you with unsolicited information! This is just like your developing a friendship with the shopkeepers at a specialty store that you frequent. They will anticipate your tastes and interests and will offer to you things that you might like. In a similar fashion, your Higher Self will begin to offer you information that you didn't even know you needed. This is just wonderful.

You might have a regular television or you may have an HDTV. You are still receiving the same TV show, only now in high definition! The input hasn't changed; however, your reception has improved greatly. Your ability to perceive the information has changed.

You are a special and powerful being. You know who you are, yet at the same time may be afraid to admit it. If you are reading this book, you know that. This does not mean that you are better than anyone else. You are NOT better. You are equal. Your role is unique. Your self-awareness may be larger than another, but it does not mean you are more evolved or better than another.

What it does mean is that you are self-aware to a different degree than someone else. The color red vibrates faster than the color blue. Does that faster vibration make red better than blue? Hardly!

You could be part of the way-showers who have arrived for the purpose of going ahead and helping others. If this is true, you will be drawn to serve as part of the enlightenment crew. Keep up the good work and you will be helping many others besides yourself!

Ask for what you need

There is lots of support from "home" for individuals who choose to do the difficult jobs. If you are reading this, chances are you are one of the strong, volunteer way-showers. You didn't come in alone. You have plenty of unseen helpers. You have plenty of support from the Creator. All you need to do is ask for the help you need. Do it daily, since this is a free-will zone and you get a clean slate every day.

Like the protagonist of the popular movie series of the 1990s, James Bond relies on his wits. He also receives plenty of support in terms of getting all the latest information and equipment that enable him to perform heroic feats.

He gets all the glory and credit, even though there is a huge body of research and science behind him that makes many of his tasks possible. He still must apply his personal ingenuity to complete the job. You must be willing to take the first step, to "step up to the plate" as they say in baseball, i.e., to do your work. You must be willing to risk failure to achieve your evolution. Ask for the help you need. The price is right, and believe me when I tell you, the beings of light are here to support you and need you to ask in order for them to fulfill their mission. Remember, we are in a free-will zone.

Bond is able to access what he needs in the moment. And so can you. One thing is certain, just because your friends and family might not provide a whole lot of positive reinforcement, that doesn't mean all of Heaven doesn't care. All of Heaven is asking you to break through the patterns of your past, your family, your generations, our society, our culture, etc. Not having support from your physical family forces you to gain conviction about what you believe and what you want. This actually helps you define boundaries and claim your power! Support is there from the heavenly hosts because you are at the front of the masses.

The Higher Self is a version of *you* that is fully connected to God. Imagine for a moment that your Higher Self is like a circuit board that has unlimited potential. With your third dimensional expression, you have a very limited circuit board. If you put too much voltage through the circuit— you can burn it out. You can try to go directly to God, but because of your circuit board's limitation, your connection to God is restricted by who you are in the physical body, your beliefs, desires and experiences. You can expand your heart to increase your capacity. As you gain experience through the many practices offered in this book, you will discover that your capacity to know and express your love of God increases dramatically, along with your Higher Self-connection.

Is there a lower self?

Yes, there is a lower self. The lower self is like the child to your adult ego self. The lower self is dedicated to keeping you safe, teaching you about the ways of the world and helping you to understand life. In a way it is the "simple" you. Up until now, the lower self has done a good job. After all, it got you this far! It is a compilation of mostly your ego and your desire body, emotional body, mental body and your physical body. It includes all the elements of you that operate your four lower body systems (physical, emotional, mental, etheric) that are centered on a physical incarnation.

The lower self is your friend

The lower self will give you accurate information, especially if it has to do with your physical safety or your emotional body. This means that your lower self will give you information that will always be correct for the immediate circumstances. This means the information is accurate, to a point. The individuals who are around you and the environment can influence the lower-self feedback. The lower self also keeps track of past hurts and wounds to help you avoid similar situations.

The lower self can also jump in and answer your questions without you realizing it is the lower self. The practice of kinesiology, or muscle testing to read the body, is lower-self information. You can get lower-self data from a pendulum as well. You might use kinesiology or a pendulum to decide what vitamins you should take, what therapies you might need or determine sensitivities to food.

I don't recommend the use of a pendulum, in general, as it can become a crutch and because your environment or the material that it is made from can influence it. Ideally you will develop a connection with your Higher Self that makes the use of the pendulum obsolete.

Remember, your goal is self-mastery and becoming your most evolved expression of you. When you access your most authentic source, your Higher Self is your direct connection to God. Lower-self information can be accurate to a point, but its operating system is based on experiences gained from living in a physical body. The lower self derives that information from your four lower bodies. It may also be pulling information and collecting data from individuals around you and from the environment. You could be influenced inappropriately by your lower self reflecting the data from your physical location or from nearby persons as well.

Because the lower self keeps track of past hurts and wounds, it can influence you to stay away from situations. Your lower self might choose to avoid similar painful situations that may be important to you now. The lower self has your best interests at heart. But it acts like a child in comparison to your Higher Self. This means that it has a limited version of what you wish for yourself in this reality. It also is not as readily able to cross-reference all of your needs into one composite understanding.

Differences between the lower self and the Higher Self

The lower self has your personal information close at hand. The Higher Self has access to all the information from the four lower bodies, your Divine Self, and other persons involved, and is able to integrate them to bring balanced responses. Your Higher Self has access to everything beyond your physical senses as well, along with everything beyond your mental awareness in the recess of your mind. When you go on a driving trip and you use your GPS (Global Positioning System) it tells you all the roadblocks and delays. Using the Higher Self is like using your GPS. This is compared with the lower self that may be reading a map, but might not have the latest updates.

The Higher Self responds to your current request, taking in all factors, known or unknown to you. Using your Higher Self ensures you are fully connected to the reality throughout all time, all dimensions and all space.

Yes, but what about intuition?

Information received intuitively can be coming from any of the above places. It may or may not include all pertinent data. Your intuitive information could also be coming from external entities, or energies that are not authentically you. Other people's thoughts can enter your head, especially if they are thinking about you, and you are thinking about them. Many couples experience this communication phenomenon as normal. Information coming from your lower self may feel like it is coming from intuition. It could come from your desires. It can come from external entities. It might come from the little person in you that wants something that you have long forgotten about. Your information might come from your angels or guides.

Angels and guides

What's wrong with getting information from the angels or guides? Nothing is wrong with that except it is not authentically you, and your purpose and goal here is to learn and gain access to your divinity. Your angels and guides stand ready to help you at any time, and are probably there with you now. The purpose of the angelic presence on earth is to help build a personal relationship between Creator and man.

They want you to gain this connection and will fully support your getting it. The angels have given me a metaphor to explain this. Suppose you are on a mountain road driving in a fun sports car. Initially you might be going pretty fast as you enjoy the open air, the sunshine and the beautiful countryside.

Real examples of using Higher Self instead of lower self

Your lower self kicks in (that's the part of you that keeps you safe most of the time), looking at the environment, deciding that maybe you should slow down and take it easy; after all it is a pretty curvy road. Maybe it's an angel telling you to slow down. Another car comes from the other way, and you manage to stay out of his way, even though he has gone left of center right in front of you! You end up swerving to your side of the road, but still safe. You manage to pull yourself together, and you think, "Wow that was a close call. Good thing I slowed down and was able to get out of the way! Good thing my reactions were so quick!" Lower self is *reactive*. *Your Higher Self is proactive.*

Your Higher Self would experience this whole scenario and take a proactive approach. Your Higher Self will be aware of the oncoming car, long before you are. Your Higher Self will send you a message such as, "Why don't you take a break? You have been driving for a while and need to rest. There is a scenic overlook coming up ahead; pull over and enjoy the view?" When the opposing car from the other direction comes down that road towards you, you find you are out of harm's way! You might not even know that a reckless driver is coming down the hill. You never notice because your Higher Self directed you to get off the road! You are able to see how your Higher Self influenced your actions *proactively* and allowed the circumstances to occur around you, while keeping you from being directly involved.

The process
Step 1—Name your practice period
Begin by making a contract with yourself for a minimum of six weeks.

This is simply a cycle of time that you agree to, from this point forward, like a gym membership. It means you show up, daily, many times a day for the six weeks or more. Ideally, take a moment now—to figure out when that date is complete—in the future. Pick any convenient date that is 45 days from now. Write it down—in your calendar or this book.

Your practice period

You want to be completely happy with your decision, so do this now. I will refer to the practice period as being six weeks for the sake of discussion. Your practice period is 45 days or more; the exact length of time is for you to decide. Specifically, if today is July 15th, your practice period will end on September 1st.

Step 2—Meditation to get Higher Self Symbols

Sit quietly for a little while with your eyes closed. Repeat this request in your thought: *Dear God, show me how much I am loved.* Repeat at least three times and wait for a feeling of expansion—usually coming from your chest. Then repeat the following to your Higher Self:

> Higher Self, I am choosing to be in my heart. Please join me in my heart.
>
> Higher Self, I am committing to build a new level of communication between me and You.
>
> Higher Self, show me a symbol or signal for "yes."
>
> Higher Self, show me a symbol for "no."
>
> Higher Self, show me a symbol for "neutral."
>
> Thank you, Higher Self, for working with me!

What's the best time to do this?

When you are able to sit quietly for at least twenty minutes! Just like a cell phone, it is far easier to receive clear communication if you are in a place with good reception! If your cell phone keeps cutting out on you, you are likely to limit your conversation until you can have clear reception. Remember that the best reception between you and your Higher Self is while you are in your heart. A woman observed in a class that everyone around her was getting guidance from his or her Higher Self, yet she wasn't.

Someone said, "Have you asked?"

Asking your Higher Self to work with you more closely will bring the Higher Self in more closely! You are also making a clear commitment to start to interact with your Higher Self. It is an important act of will. Make sure you ask!

What would a signal from the Higher Self look like? How do I know that I am getting a real signal?

A signal or symbol from the Higher Self can take on any form. For those of you who are kinesthetic, you will experience a feeling; some have a sense or a knowing. Others get colors, or shapes, or other visual experiences; some will hear something; others will have a scent appear. Uri Geller used kinetic energy to bend a fork. Feeling the river of connection widen for you, if you already have this sense or feeling, will come with practice.

What if I don't get Yes and No symbols or signals?

If you have asked your Higher Self for symbols or signals and you come up with nothing, then it is time for you to select symbols that you can understand and then teach them to your Higher Self. You will need to pick something to communicate this knowledge of what you want for the signal or symbol for "yes," "no," and "neutral."

How do I teach the Higher Self my signals?

What if I don't get a clear signal in meditation? Now what do I do? When my oldest son was a two-year-old, he taught us the word for cheese; it was "ga." He couldn't say cheese, so every time he saw cheese, a favorite of his at the time, he named it for us. We learned that if he wanted cheese, he would say, "ga." If your Higher Self doesn't give you a clear signal, then you will assign a value to "yes" and "no" that you can recognize in this same way.

To set the matrix for "yes" and "no" signals, select something that you can easily replicate in your mind's eye. Make it something simple that you will accept. For example, if you see colors easily, red could stand for "no," and green for "yes," or thumbs up for "yes," thumbs down for "no."

If you are more of a "feeling" or kinesthetic type individual, you may find it easier to experience energy in your body or a feeling. You might decide that a simple energy "whoosh" on the right side could stand for "yes," and on the left for "no," and in the middle for "neutral." Pick something that will work for you. But PICK SOMETHING and let it stand. Don't question it.

If you decide that a red car should be your signal for "yes," and you close your eyes, and can't imagine a red car, then that is not a good signal for you. You must select something that you can replicate in your mind's eye, and then your Higher Self can communicate it to you to experience it. Then practice with something you already know the answer to so that you can get the feel of it. Such as, "Do I have one son?" You already know the answer. Let the correct symbol or signal present itself. Continue practicing with mundane things like, "Should I wear this or that shirt today, or should I take this route or the 'back' route to work?" Looking at a menu ask, "Soup?" If the response is "neutral," ask, "Salad?" If the response is "neutral," ask, "Both?" The response is "yes." Remember to phrase them as yes or no questions.

Examples of symbols or signals

Brian's "yes" symbol is a smiley face. When he went walking on the beach right after the meditation where that information came in, he found a rock with a smiley face carved into it by Mother Nature. The synchronicity of finding that shell was the Higher Self providing clarity and reinforcing his signal.

Kelly first experienced her Higher Self through the Michelangelo painting of the hand of God reaching for the hand of man as her symbol of the Higher Self. Her "yes" signal was a thumb pointing up, and thumbs down for "no." Dennis's Higher Self has a sense of humor. His signals are a Mickey Mouse white-gloved hand with the thumbs up or down for "yes" and "no" respectively.

A man in the class was the "drag along" partner of a woman who was very into this work. He decided to attend on a whim. He had never really done any meditation before. He asked me, in a whispered voice, "Can your Higher Self have a sense of humor?" When the Higher Self connection was made, his Higher Self showed him a red beating heart for "yes" and green M&Ms for "no!" That same man was given a vision of his Higher Self the following day. He whispered in my ear, "Can my Higher Self be a woman?" That same man shares the same first name with another of the students from a few years back. Both men's Higher Selves appear as a woman!

In one class there was a lot of crystal energy expressed in this location, and the store hosting me had hundreds of crystals. Many participants in this class experienced their signals in the form of crystals. In another class a man, Tom, was a former military guy. His signals reflected him as a paratrooper getting ready to jump from a plane! His "neutral" signal was him at the open door of the plane and he never jumps. His "no" signal is the jump and his parachute doesn't open. "Yes" is him jumping and the chute opens! Another man in that same class sees his Higher Self represented by lightning. Jagged means "yes" and has a direct feeling. Spiral lightning is "no" with a dancing type feeling and "neutral" shows up as a flat line of lightning.

Neutral

The signal for "neutral" frequently tends to come up as a flat line, or some variation thereof, such as a horizon, the sea or a minus sign. The next table contains some of the information from students coming through the meditation where I introduce the Higher Self and ask for the Higher Self signals.

Help! I'm not getting anything!

Many people experience shapes such as triangles, circles, tetrahedrons, etc., as one of their signals. If you don't get a symbol or signal—don't despair. You are not alone, and I'll be providing tools to help you with your Higher Self communication. If you don't get a signal, then it just means you aren't visual or auditory. It may mean that you are so mental or cerebral that you haven't "allowed" those signals to appear for you. Allow yourself to see or feel any kind of response, and with practice, you will find the Higher Self connection.

In the next chapter you will receive instructions and techniques to help you develop and strengthen your Higher Self-connection. Practice is critical.

What kinds of questions will you ask during your practice period?

This is perhaps one of the most critical sections on how to work with your Higher Self. You will choose questions that have no value to you, and are of no consequence to you. These questions will be about things that you really don't care which way you do it.

The reason you ask about insignificant things is because you do not want your ego to participate. Your ego has done a terrific job of getting you where you are today, and it won't be able to resist participating on issues you care about. So give yourself a break from the ego, and select questions that the ego doesn't care about.

For example, you might ask, "Should I wear the red shirt or the blue shirt?" If you are meeting your best friend who always compliments how you look when wearing red, then you probably would want to wear the red shirt, and so it is not a good practice question.

Ask questions you are willing to follow through on, regardless

Make sure that your practice period is loaded with questions that you are willing to ask, and follow through on, no matter what your Higher Self tells you! If you are unwilling to follow through with the Higher Self answer, then don't ask it!

If you love pizza, then don't ask your Higher Self if you should eat it, because the temptation to eat one would be too great. You might decide to eat it, and then later tell yourself, "Well, the 'no' really wasn't a clear signal, and I really couldn't tell." You don't want to sabotage yourself; so don't ask Higher Self questions if you already prefer the outcome a certain way.

If you ask your Higher Self a question, and then decide not to follow it, you will be sabotaging your practice. During the practice period, please remember, if you ask your Higher Self, you must follow through. If you don't, then you will interfere with your communication and defeat the purpose of your practice period, which is to develop this spectacular connection.

Why is my ego eliminated in this equation?

Your ego has done a great job of getting you this far. Your ego won't easily relinquish the job of running your life. Your ego doesn't need you asking your Higher Self for things that it used to handle for you. This is why there is so much hesitation and uncertainty among so many people about messages that come in. You are very likely getting great information from your guides and Higher Self, but then your ego, who has managed all of this input for you in the past, gets in the middle and you begin to doubt and re-think!

In fact, your ego may have been instrumental in influencing your buying and reading this book that led you to this point. Your ego wants you to be happy. Your ego wants you to get what you have determined is important (i.e., information, knowledge, understanding and more). Your ego collects its information from the lower self and the world around you.

Imagine for a moment that your ego is a really good Administrative Assistant (AA). Your AA does a wonderful job of making appointments, purchasing, organizing, setting up your business meetings and managing your day. Your ego is like that. Next, imagine the reaction you would get if you told your AA that you were going to handle all the appointments, purchasing, business meetings and organizing. She wouldn't like it and might ask, "Is there a problem with my performance? I've done a great job for you so far. Are you trying to eliminate me?"

If, however, you told your AA you would start taking out the trash, she would reply, "Great! Take the one under my desk first since it gets filled the fastest." If you tell her you will start washing the windows, she will tell you that the ones in reception need it the most and to do those first. Why? She doesn't want those jobs anyway. Your ego will not resist your Higher Self communication by selecting things that you (or your ego) don't care about! This is an easy way to learn the language of the Higher Self. If you are a control freak and need to decide everything, then you will have to pay extra attention to this.

For example, some people know exactly what they want to wear, exactly what they are going to eat, and manage even the most mundane details of their life with great precision. If this is you, decide now what you are willing to "negotiate." Find out what you are willing to ask your Higher Self and then use that short list every day. "Which route do I take to work?" "Should I use the Stairmaster or the running machine?" "Should I fix green beans or spinach for dinner?" Then sit back and watch the magic.

Maybe you prefer to run in the morning but you get a "yes" for "Stairmaster." You get on the Stairmaster machine and watch someone else get on the treadmill. Your envy turns into appreciation when you see that the treadmill isn't working. It was the same one you would have used! Little by little the seeds of faith and knowing get planted. Within the practice period of 45 days you will have enough synchronicity to know with great certainty the very real tangible benefit of your Higher Self communication.

At some point your ego is looking at all of these wonderful synchronicities and starts to see that you will get everything (happiness, knowledge, understanding, etc.) if you ask your Higher Self to decide!

Full integration of the Higher Self

In reality, you are integrating the ego into your Higher Self so that your Higher Self is God's Will. It is a powerful place to be—to be so fully connected to your Higher Self that you are always operating from your "fifth-dimensional self" (5D). We will explain 5D in a later section of this book. Ultimately, what you are doing is weaving the Higher Self and the ego together, so that your ego wants what your Higher Self offers you, because the benefit is clear. Your practice period gives your ego the proof!

I am not one of the teachers who believes the ego must be subdued. Instead, I believe the ego can be integrated into the Higher Self and vice versa, creating "one will," God's Will.

Later, after your practice period is complete and your Higher Self-connection is crystal clear—it is ok to not "do what your Higher Self" tells you. I'm laughing as I write this, because when you test this out a few months from now, you will realize once your Higher Self tells you any answer, you will regret not following it. Furthermore, in all cases that I know of, the Higher Self-connection will always insist and persist if it is critical, so no worries there. I only did this once and will write about what happened later in the book. I was sorry, too.

Remember, if you don't think you can go either way regarding something your Higher Self tells you to do, then don't ask. This is a perfect indication that you have an attachment to the outcome and that it is not a good Higher Self question for you during your practice time.

This is not about belief

Asking "why?" serves the ego. Belief involves understanding, which still relies on the ego. Being-ness relies on knowingness.

So it's not important to believe in your Higher Self. Trust will follow after you have blindly followed your Higher Self signals for six weeks. Your practice will develop confidence and that will lead to trust. It is about knowing that your Higher Self makes it possible for you to be in the MOMENT.

In the case of Higher Self questions, you choose to rely on the feedback that comes in. This means that you do not worry about whether you get immediate feedback about the choice and whether it was the perfect one or not. You will wait for some lovely synchronicity to give you feedback that shows the accuracy of your communication.

For example, when you call a friend for lunch and he agrees to meet, you might ask where he wants to go. He doesn't care and offers, "You pick, I chose last time." So you ask your Higher Self because you don't care either. You ask, "Chinese or Pizza?" You ask your Higher Self each one, yes or no. Both answers should validate each other. Your Higher Self picks pizza, and while you're there you run into someone you had been trying to connect with for months. Here the Universe is giving you the synchronicity and reinforcement that lets you know you are getting good information from your Higher Self.

Remember, you must agree to follow whatever your Higher Self gives you during your practice period. If, during your practice period, you ask your Higher Self a question, and then you decide not to follow it, you will sabotage your language skills.

Be aware of the types of questions you are asking

One man I worked with told me that he was still having trouble with the Higher Self answers. I asked what kind of questions he was asking, and he said that he would ask his Higher Self if the traffic light in front of him would turn green before he got to it. I remember laughing and stating, "You still care about the answer!" and he replied, "No, I really don't care if the light is red or green."

And I replied, "Yes, but you are looking for immediate feedback that proves that you are right!"

He said, "No, I really don't care whether I get home five minutes later."

As an engineer, he felt it was his responsibility to track his Higher Self's accuracy. What he is doing is keeping score. He thinks it is necessary in order to make sure the Higher Self is coming through. He is an engineer and, of course, believes that he has to collect this data. While it is true you are to collect data, you must not seek immediate feedback. Instead, wait for synchronicity to provide the data to prove your Higher Self-connection.

If you practice basketball, you might stand in front of the basketball hoop, aiming and shooting dozens of times. At each opportunity you aim for the basket. You focus on getting the ball into the basket. You keep adjusting your aim based upon the feedback of where the ball went, compared to what you did before. If you were shooting hoops, you would use the feedback to improve your aim each time you missed. With the Higher Self practice you do not look for immediate feedback. If you do, you are likely to dismiss the correct answers as lucky guesses, and the wrong ones with, "See, it doesn't work."

If you keep looking for feedback to get the evidence that your Higher Self was right, you have not totally detached from the practice questions. The purpose of this exercise is to learn to allow your Higher Self to communicate, so implicitly that your ego will observe and conclude that this is a good thing. Ultimately, your goal is to incorporate your ego with your Higher Self so perfectly that the two become integrated into one will, God's Will.

Unifying with God's Will

Asking unimportant questions means you are not tracking the results. It is the very "not tracking" that produces this "not caring" attitude so very necessary to your success. As you let go of the need to evaluate or be right, your Higher Self will be able to give you enough evidence, with the 50 or more daily questions, that the results will become irrefutable.

Remember, it's important to choose questions that you have no attachment to the outcome. Any sort of predictive question meant that the engineer would know instantly if his Higher Self was right or wrong. When he was right, he would compare it to all the wrong answers and conclude this whole Higher Self thing wasn't working. Scorekeeping isn't allowed during your practice period. Instead, let the synchronicities produce the score!

Your job during the practice period is to keep your ego out of the action. Taking your ego out of the action means that you decide to have no interest in whether your Higher Self is accurate initially, and use the passive positive feedback to reinforce your signals.

"I ask my Higher Self a question but I never get an answer."

If you don't get an answer to the question, "Is this my Higher Self telling me something?" consider the possibility that your Higher Self did not advise you like you think it did. Perhaps it is other forces within you. "Hmm, yes, well, I'm an external entity that you picked up in a bar the other day, and I told you to sleep with that person." Be specific and confirm that it was your Higher Self giving you the answer.

Have you ever heard the answer to, "Who ate the last cookie in the cookie jar?" Of course not. No one will answer that question! Who or what inside of you is going to volunteer that?

Folks, it's not going to happen! The point is, if there is an entity in you urging you to take some action, or your lower self is wishing for some preferred outcome, you may think it is your Higher Self when it isn't. When you ask the question, "Is this my Higher Self telling me to (fill in the blank)?" and you do not get your well-practiced "yes" signal, that is the answer. This lack of a "yes" signal is proof it is NOT your Higher Self leading you into this action. This is important to remember. The absence of a clear signal means it is NOT your Higher Self that was advising you in that moment.

The only way to know for sure, especially when you are in a dilemma and you are really wondering, is to ask, "Is this my Higher Self telling me to do this?" This bears repeating. Only your Higher Self is permitted to answer, "Yes."

Cosmic law: only your Higher Self is permitted to answer "yes" to the question, "Is this my Higher Self telling me this?"

When you are in a place where you are filled with doubt, or emotional questioning or emotional suffering, ask your Higher Self to validate your information. Only your Higher Self will be able to answer "yes" to the question, "Is this my Higher Self telling me (fill in the blank)?" This is Cosmic Law. If you are having trouble with this, try rebalancing your energy by asking your Higher Self to show you your "yes" signal and your "no" signal and your "neutral" signal. This will neutralize the field. Then ask the question again.

Please be very careful. Your Higher Self will never tell you to do something that is dishonest or immoral. Your Higher Self will never justify any action that would hurt another. If you are suspicious of an answer that you get from your Higher Self, you can ask again. When in doubt, do without.

How do you achieve proficiency?

Promise yourself that you will keep this commitment to ask your Higher Self as many mundane, ordinary, unimportant or insignificant questions you can think of each day during your six-week trial. I suggest you ask practice questions 50 times or more each day. Your Higher Self won't mind. What kinds of questions are considered mundane? Anything you don't have an attachment to. If you love a particular candy like bon-bons, even though it is not a major question of life, then it probably isn't a good question to ask your Higher Self about eating them!

What kind of questions will you ask?

Is it in my highest and best good to:

- Wear the red shirt or the blue one?
- Follow this route or that one to work?
- Skip dinner?
- Call someone now?
- Go to the gym today? Now?
- Fix the carrots or the cucumbers for dinner?

If your dinner guest loves carrots, then you may already have decided on cooking carrots to please your guest. Just cook the carrots and don't ask during your six-week trial.

On the other hand, if you don't have a plan for dinner guests, and you ask this question, and the response is to cook carrots, then do it. Then when the doorbell rings, and the surprise visitor who ends up staying for dinner happens to love carrots, you can thank your Higher Self for knowing this before you started cooking!

No exceptions

During this practice period please refrain from asking your Higher Self questions that are exceptionally important. This is to make sure that you are not jeopardizing your practice period with issues you are attached to! If you need to make an important decision that is time sensitive and you need to use your Higher Self, please do. But this should be a rare exception. Kindly postpone every significant question you possibly can until your practice period has been completed.

When your practice period is completed, you will start asking open-ended questions. We suggest you review this again, once your practice period is completed.

To recap, there are seven basic rules for your Higher Self practice period.

THE SEVEN RULES FOR HIGHER SELF CONNECTION

1. *Select a timeframe. This is called your practice period. It should be no less than 45 days. It could be longer. Decide what your practice period future end date is. If today is July 1, then August 15 is the end of your practice period.*

2. *Ask ONLY yes or no questions. No open-ended questions.*

3. *Ask unimportant, insignificant questions that you do not care what the outcome will be, such as, "Should I take this route to get to work?" or "Should I wear the red shirt?" Keep asking new questions (about what to wear) until you get a "yes." Ask unimportant questions throughout the day as often as 30-50 times.*

4. *Always follow through on your answer. No exceptions. This is to keep the practice period clear. After your practice period, if you decide not to follow your Higher Self, it is ok—but you will probably regret it.*

5. *Do not ask important questions. If you absolutely cannot defer asking this question until after your 45 days, then make an exception. Make exceptions rare.*

6. *Do not ask predictive questions such as, "Will the traffic light change before I get there?" or "Will the phone ring in the next few minutes?" These type questions are inviting your ego to track your progress. If you are tracking your progress, then you still care about the outcome. (See Rule #3.)*

7. *Do not use any forms of divination during your practice period. Do not use kinesiology, muscle testing, finger testing, cards or pendulums. Divination has its place and can be useful but not during your practice period. If you are a therapist and use these methods with your patients, limit their use to that practice. As far as YOU are concerned, you are only asking your Higher Self during this practice period.*

Learning the language of "non-judgment"

How do you learn this language? Ask your Higher Self to work with you in achieving this awareness. Although it isn't natural by normal standards of "mass consciousness," you can acquire it with practice. Approach it like any change of habits. Perhaps, when you were younger, you used to use slang words, and now you don't because they don't give you the results they used to. It is a bit like that.

If you have been in a class with me, you know we practice re-framing judgmental statements. For example, if you ask your daughter to stop being cruel to your house guests, you are actually locking her into that behavior by asking her to NOT do that. Instead, you might say ask her to be kind to everyone who lives here because, "That is how we do things in our house." Notice that this statement doesn't state your daughter's behavior is good or bad, yet clearly conveys a different behavior is required.

Open-ended questions are for after your practice period

Open-ended questions are questions that could have any answer. Typically they are the opposite of yes/no questions. You can ask your Higher Self any open-ended question. Who did that? When will my son understand? Why is such and such happening? One time I asked my Higher Self why my van was making a certain noise, and surprised even myself with the precise answer that I had no reason to know or understand!

Developing mastery with certain kinds of questions

I discourage you from asking your Higher Self questions so you can make a decision about something. It is more appropriate to ask your Higher Self what you should do in a situation. For example, instead of asking your Higher Self if someone you do not care to see is going to be at a party so you can decide whether or not to attend, ask if it's in your highest and best good to be at that party this night. It is never advisable to ask your Higher Self about a situation and then make a decision. That action is ego driven.

At a certain level your Higher Self will start giving you unsolicited information. This is the ultimate. If you develop a rapport with an expert who lives near you, at some point in the friendship he will offer information you have not requested. Actively soliciting your Higher Self many times during your practice period will open the gate and keep it wide open for information to flow in both directions freely and because the friendship and connection implies your interest and advice.

The logical reason for following your Higher Self

I always followed my Higher Self knowing it is worthwhile; however, I desired to provide proof for those who were new to this arena. Knowing vs. trusting the Higher Self could make a huge difference in deciding to always follow your Higher Self.

For months I meditated on this question. I was obsessed with finding a logical reason to follow your Higher Self unwaveringly. I understood this question would be useful to logical, type A personalities. I knew many individuals would benefit from a logical reason for always following your Higher Self.

One morning the answer came as I was coming out of the dreamtime. I was seeing a local weather report as it interrupted a movie on TV. Why do we listen to this interrupt? The weather is about to change dramatically. Logic tells us that when a weather report interrupts local programming, there is an impending change in the weather. It tells us this situation that appears normal is about to change drastically. If hail is suddenly expected, you may want to put your car in the garage. It's a warning to "take action now."

Once your Higher Self communication is strong and flowing easily in both directions, the logical reason to always follow your Higher Self is that your Higher Self will communicate with you in advance of when you need to know something or do something. Having this "advance notice system" that is always turned on and communicating with you allows you to quell the voice of logic that may be telling you something different. This is because your Higher Self is providing you with an interruption of "local normal" with an update to inform you that things are not "normal" as they appear! Once you commit to always follow your Higher Self, it will be second nature for you to follow through.

Knowledge is power

Save yourself hundreds of hours of effort by understanding this simple principle. One day, in Asheville, NC, I had a class where a builder who owned his own contracting business complained his wife lost her cell phone. He said she lost it four months ago and that she was sure she lost it in his truck! They took everything out—seats, carpet and tools—looking for that missing phone. In the end he had to give her his cell phone and he got a new one. He said to me, "What do you say?"

I repeated, "If my wife's cell phone is in the fourth dimension I'd like it back. Thank you."

He repeated after me and added, "I'm driving for lunch today!" At the lunch break he opened the front door of his cab. I was on the passenger side just as quickly. We both wanted to see what would happen. He reached in under the seat and pulled out his wife's missing cell phone! He looked at me and said, "If this had not happened to me personally, I would not have believed you!"

What's going on?

You will learn more about the "fourth dimension" in my other books. Ultimately, I concluded that there is only one question to ask your Higher Self. That question is non-pejorative, non-judgmental and very open ended. It is, "Higher Self, what is going on?"

Now, the *opening of your heart is the key* to understanding the information you are getting. Think of your heart opening as if it were a translator. The more open and receptive to giving and receiving unconditional love, the more you will be able to translate the data that is coming in. The more experienced your heart is in practicing unconditional love, the more incoming information will be meaningful to you. There is a direct relationship between your heart and your understanding. If it is knowledge you seek, then open your heart to get the answer.

To learn the maximum amount of understandable information, one simply asks the question with no bias. The question that reflects no bias is, "Higher Self, what's going on?" I suggest you use this formula every time something happens that defies the rules of reality.

To increase your efforts' success

Start asking the Higher Self how much you are loved. Ask your Higher Self, "Higher Self, show me how much I am loved!" This is so powerful, and so significant, that I recommend that you ask your Higher Self this question every single day. It is especially important when you are working at the pioneering level, clearing out painful emotional issues no matter what the subject or venue. This, along with the Hathor Toning (found in *Mantras for Ascension* CD), gives you a leg up on doing the meditation by yourself. Add this to your daily practice and watch your heart heal in ways you didn't even know were needed. In my Advanced Flower of Life Workshop, we have had many examples of what happens to individuals when they ask this question, and I would like to share a few.

One doctor said that when she asked her Higher Self to tell her how much she was loved, she saw first one beautiful rose, in pink, then several roses, and then hundreds of roses, and the colors kept increasing, finally representing the entire spectrum of the rainbow. In the space between the roses, the light began to glow gradually. This glow began to get brighter and brighter. The whole thing gave her this feeling of soft, nurturing support.

You must begin to ask questions that are truly non-judgmental. You do not care if you can verify at the ego level or any other level. The verification will percolate up from within the environment—from sources inside and outside you. I call them synchronicities.

Just like the marksman continues to increase the range of difficulty, you can now increase the "level of difficulty" in your non-attached questions to include non-attachment as to "how" they are verified!

Notice that when the engineer was trying to get Higher Self signals, it didn't work for him; yet, later when he wasn't working on it, so intensely they came in. His clear intent allowed that to occur. If you are like this engineer, and have a very logical way of thinking and adapting to change, you will need to allow yourself the space and let go of data collection first!

This means you must allow your Higher Self to communicate with you—without your usual record keeping. You must lighten up your scientific thinking into a more playful approach. This is one of the reasons author Drunvalo Melchizedek said you must be like a child. This will give you the breathing room necessary for your Higher Self to shine through. As your practice develops, you will notice the value of the Higher Self-connection. Challenge your desire to evaluate this before your 45 days of practice! Let the evidence weigh in at the end of the experiment.

Advanced questions after your practice period is complete

After 45 days from your start date.

What if I ask my Higher Self about something and then decide I don't want to do it?

Your Higher Self is not a parent. It will not correct you or save you from your mistakes. Fortunately your Higher Self does not sit in judgment of your activities. It doesn't decide that you were wrong or bad because you asked a Higher Self question and then didn't follow through.

In my opinion, if you don't follow your Higher Self, you will be sorry! I did not follow my Higher Self only one time. True to the above, I was sorry! While teaching in New York I proposed getting together with some dear friends who lived there. The only night I had available, they had already made plans to see a movie. I checked in to see if I was supposed to see the movie. Nope. I really wanted to see my friends, so against the answer my Higher Self had given me, I went to the movie anyway, just so I could be with my friends. The movie was so bad I wanted to walk out. They thought the same thing! None of us wanted to be there, but all of us suffered through that awful movie for concern of hurting the others' feelings! What a waste! Now I know better.

I can promise you that if you ask your Higher Self, you will get the best answer that will please every aspect of you, even the ones you don't know about or think about. Your ego might not think so in the moment, but hindsight is a great teacher! Your Higher Self has all your priorities and aspects in full view and is giving you an informed answer! The answer is the exact answer you would give yourself if you knew everything, and your Higher Self does!

Become the humble servant. Become the fool to Spirit. Give yourself permission to "hear what is going on." Once you have learned to step out of judgment, then you will be open to the messages of the Universe all the time. The daily practice of meditation will help you clear your judgments, wounds and fears. Get in the habit of asking in this non-judgmental way, "What is going on?" You will be amazed at the answers that will start coming. Remember your practice period is completed for this.

Connecting to the Higher Self comes through this process that is highly effective and accurate. I encourage you to use this practice to develop your own consistency. Your practice will be the best investment you have ever made aside from my original FOL workshop. This specific practice, as detailed here, will enable you to achieve 100 percent accuracy with your Higher Self. After your practice period, you may start asking this and other "open-ended" questions. If you are serious about developing a connection with your Higher Self that is virtually foolproof, you will need to practice. You will choose to practice with questions that have no consequence to you.

The Universe rearranges itself to accommodate your picture of reality. What are you fascinated by? This is what the Universe works on. The goal then becomes being the master of Divine expression. It means no limitation! We are not locked into physical reality. We are becoming Light from within. We are no longer looking to an outside authority. Remember, what do you do when something happens that defies explanation? Ask your Higher Self, "What's going on?" For further information *www.MaureenStGermain.com*.

YOU HAVE A MULTIDIMENSIONAL LIFE PURPOSE

Suzanne Strisower

"Before I can tell my life what I want to do with it,
I must listen to my life telling me who I am."
—Peter Palmer

Living multidimensionally

Every person is a living breathing hologram, and one that is made up of many different components of energy and self. From a multidimensional perspective, we operate in several different aspects of consciousness simultaneously—what I call 3/4/5D living. There are many other dimensions, but these are the ones that most relate to our lives today. We all need to learn how to be conscious in these dimensions. The "3D" is our common day-to-day world of DOING and the activities of our daily lives. Our "4D" reality is connected to the unseen world and our intuition, it guides us in what direction to go, shows us our higher calling, and gives us our KNOWING. The next level of evolutionary consciousness that we are all evolving toward is "5D," BEING, the mystical, vibrational or essential aspects of ourselves that we experience when we are in the flow. A great poem that reflects this multidimensionality is from Stephen Levine's book, *Who Dies*:

> *"Buddha left a road map,*
> *Jesus left a road map,*
> *Krishna left a road map,*
> *Rand McNally left a road map.*
> *But you still have to travel the road yourself."*

On the planet, our task right now is to realign with our beings and the place of creation that flows into our guidance to have our knowingness lead us into right action and right livelihood. Often, clients ask me, "How do you do that?" I always recommend starting within—start with your life purpose. Our life's purpose is also 3/4/5D and multidimensional; it begins with our mystical 5D purpose, how we just BE, our Spirit or divine spark of God embodied. The mystical purpose is about aliveness and consciousness.

This consciousness gives us a sense of itself in 4D through our awareness and KNOWING, when our intuition and inner guidance kicks in and we sense and feel things that we can't see; we only know through our various extra-sensory abilities to perceive. We get downloads from this place which tell us how to act, what to do, or what direction to go.

The ACTION required is something we came here to DO, which is totally in alignment with the cosmic plan that we are a part of. Living from this place means that we live a life of guidance and grace where we experience the flow of life, things move, change and evolve, and we stay in the flow of our knowing and being.

Living multidimensionally is exciting, fun and a great blessing because life is literally consciously flowing through you. You are part of the journey from a place of action, knowing, and being. Our life's purposes are similarly multidimensional when looked at holistically.

First, let's start with a definition of life purpose that is simple and complete. *Life purpose is defined simply as the "aim or intention of the energy you put forth."* It is the underlying reason why you do the things you do, I call it your "Personal WHY™." It can be teased out using a unique, holistic, and multidimensional approach.

The multidimensional aspects of our life purpose

Each of us has a multidimensional life purpose made up of 3/4/5D through the "7 Universal Life Purpose Elements" of purpose. In understanding the multidimensional system of 3/4/5D, it translates into these seven aspects:

3D—The DOINGNESS of Life—our active daily lives include these Stages of Purpose:

LIFE PURPOSE ELEMENT #1: DEVELOPMENTAL

This is structured around Maslow's Hierarchy of Needs, which are about our evolutionary mastering of this world. *What stage are you in?*

Security—Are you just starting out in life and wanting the security of a paycheck and looking for a stable job, or have you had some setbacks in life that have brought you back to *square one?* This stage is where you are just looking to get your basic needs of food, clothing and shelter met.

Stability—Are you wanting a full-time job or career and to be in control of your own destiny? You've had plenty of jobs and experience and now you want to start your career and take your life seriously. This is often where college graduates find themselves, wanting to have a *real* job and get their lives launched. This is also the phase that adults who have gone through a midlife crisis or other setback find themselves in as they start to rebuild their lives.

Social—Are you wanting to expand out into your world? The hallmark of this phase is that you now have stability and security, and you want to broaden your horizons. During this phase people want to settle down and start a family, have a long-term committed relationship, and be part of work groups or teams where you feel good about participating in something bigger than yourself and have an impact.

Self-Esteem—Are you at the point in your life where you have some mastery or expertise in some area of your life that you now want to use and capitalize on? This phase is where people who have been in careers for decades, and done something well that they have mastered, often find themselves. They are all wanting to know what is next and wondering what direction to go. The interesting thing about this stage is people get antsy; they want to expand and use what they know in some more challenging and meaningful ways. It's time to strike out on your own and let your knowledge, wisdom and expertise guide you.

Self-Actualization—Are you wanting a connection with something bigger than yourself at a spiritual or legacy level? This is a soul-searching phase where people have accomplished a lot and been very "successful," yet they experience life with a sense of *something is missing* or they want to tap into something bigger than themselves. This is where deep spiritual practices are born to get that connection with a more expanded reality.

Every person attempts to move through these five major Developmental Stages of Purpose during their lifetimes. Sometimes, we will have advanced in one of the Developmental Stages like Self-Actualization, then need to start our lives again, like people who choose a spiritual path and then leave all of their material possessions behind.

What this shows you is what your actions will be geared to accomplishing, i.e., I need to find a job (Security); I want a job that I can be in for five years (Stability); I'm wanting to find a better job or one that suits me (Social); I've been working in this industry for the past twenty years and now I want to be a consultant or coach and share my wisdom and expertise with others (Self-Esteem); or I really want to know me better and have a deeper connection with Spirit (Self-Actualization).

Which Developmental Stage of Purpose most resonates with where you are in your life right now?

_____

_____

_____

LIFE PURPOSE ELEMENT #2: PSYCHOLOGICAL

This element reflects our personality structure and what makes us tick. This involves things like whether you are an introvert or extrovert, what roles do you typically play in life, and the archetypal parts of your personality like: are you a peacemaker, homemaker, perfectionist, healer, leader, cheerleader, pioneer, magician, orphan, king, queen, etc.?

What roles do you like to play and what roles are you most comfortable playing? This tells you something about the "HOW" of your life purpose. Carol Pearson's book, *The Hero Within*, describes the following archetypes that people can be:

> *Orphan*—wants authority to give them answers (this person would make a great company employee.)
>
> *Martyr*—learns or foregoes learning for others (this person would make a great helper, social worker, someone in a volunteer capacity or non-profit.)
>
> *Wanderer*—explores new ideas in their own way (this person would be a great inventor, pioneer, public speaker, someone who is very hands-on in their own world.)
>
> *Warrior*—learns through competition and achievement (this person would be great in sales, marketing or other competitive positions.)
>
> *Magician*—allows curiosity, learns in a group or alone, wants it to be fun (this person could be a mid-level manager, or CEO like the people who run Ben & Jerry's or Zappo's shoes.)

There are many archetypal systems. Oprah created an online assessment to determine your "Striving Style," which articulates the seven different types of people:

- Striving to Help
- Striving to Be Recognized

- Striving to Be Spontaneous
- Striving to Be Knowledgeable
- Striving to Be Secure
- Striving to Be in Control

Each type can find its own expression in any profession; the key is to know what role you are most suited to play and to find a position that matches the profile. The bottom line is that each person has a particular "Psychological Purpose."

What are those aspects of your personality that you know about yourself?

_____

_____

_____

LIFE PURPOSE ELEMENT #3: PROFESSIONAL

This is the most common type of life purpose people think about when they are thinking about their 3D purpose—"what you do." It takes into account a person's skills, gifts and talents, which actually include some of the special gifts that you were born with, skills that are things that you developed, and some of the special talents that are things that you have mastered as a result of your gifts and skills. Your skills might be that you know how to paint beautiful portraits; your talent (specialty) is portraits of animals and people's pets.

Think about what the gifts are that you came into this lifetime with—what did you do well as a child? What did you love as a child? These are your innate gifts, the things you can easily do that don't require any effort. Then contemplate what you developed—what interests did you have that you acquired or honed into marketable skills, like having agility and being a great motocross rider, dancer, gymnast? Finally, what special talents do you have that often come out of your passions?

Write down what your special gifts, skills and talents are and how you most like to express them:

_____

_____

_____

LIFE PURPOSE ELEMENT #4: TRANSITIONAL

Often we find ourselves in times of change—sometimes planned, sometimes not. Each change gives us the opportunity to bring ourselves back into the present and ask ourselves, "Who am I now and what is important to me TODAY?"; or, "How would I like to express my purpose in life in the future?" These changes can be the result of an illness, death, loss of a job; or, on the positive side, wanting a change, or having reached a plateau and trying to figure out what to do next. To find your Transitional Purpose ask yourself and answer this question:

What is important to you now and WHY?

_____

_____

_____

I have people do their 3D "download and dump" so that everything they know about themselves is out on the table. Then people are curious and open to explore their 4/5D elements of purpose.

4D—KNOWING what you are here to do via your guidance

LIFE PURPOSE ELEMENT #5: NATAL

Each of us was born at a particular time and place that creates a "cosmic blueprint" for the energies that are imprinted within us from the cosmos. The Natal element also takes into account your name and its vibration and numerological significance. This is often referred to as your "destiny or purpose" number. Do a free online astrological natal chart to understand more about your sun sign and the energies that were present at your birth. Compare this with the information that you receive when you do an online numerological reading for your name and birth date.

What the major cosmic influences that I was born under are:

_____

_____

_____

LIFE PURPOSE ELEMENT #6: SPIRITUAL

This knowledge and insight are reflected through your inner guidance, dreams, intuition, higher calling, inner calling, or whatever way the divine and higher power brings wisdom to you. This is one of the most powerful expressions of our purpose because we are manifesting something from a higher power through ourselves.

Think about the tools that you use to connect and receive information from the higher dimensional realms—what have they shared with you about your purpose? What have they guided you to be doing? These are the things that you might want to explore expressing and creating.

What are the things you've been asked to bring into form or make happen in this dimension?

_____

_____

_____

5D—Being the vibration of who you truly are as an embodied Spirit

LIFE PURPOSE ELEMENT #7: MYSTICAL

The most profound of all of the purposes, because it is infused with your being, is experienced by each of us without the filters of our egos. We have a direct experience of our mystical purposes when we have a peak experience, a profound loss that "shakes us to the core of our beings," or when we are in deep meditative states or 100 percent present in the moment, where we are so engrossed in what we are doing that "we lose track of time." Think about a recent instance where time stood still, and you were in the presence of something energetic that engulfed you, something that had control over you. Nature is something that can engulf and captivate us. What insights or direction were you shown about your life, and how you were to proceed or what you were to do?

What "showed up for you"?

_____

_____

_____

Your Life Purpose DNA

All 7 Universal Elements of your multidimensional purpose, comprise the composite of who you are. They provide a direction for your life that I call your Life Purpose DNA. I recommend making a list, collage, vision board or some expression of this hologram of your being. Notice what comes through for you in some way through each of the life purpose elements.

What is showing up consistently? The underlying intent or drive is your life purpose. Some people may not have that level of clarity, so when you can't figure out the direction or dimension, start with one of two approaches. First start with 5D—what does your being want to do? This truth is the most exalted and truest, but it can also be the most confronting and revealing. The other approach is to start where you feel most comfortable and work from that place to expand into your multidimensional nature and purpose. Every person is multidimensional and has a multidimensional purpose to tap into.

What dimension are you most comfortable in now?

3D—in Action
4D—in Knowing
5D—in Being

How can you reconcile yourself to flow easily through all of the dimensions to give your Being more space? Open up and expand into that.

Once you know your Life Purpose DNA, the next step is to create a Life Purpose—Personal Mission Statement. You want your statement to be something that resonates with you multidimensionally. Here's an example:

"My life purpose is to connect humanity with the divine in practical ways so that their conscious vibration will fulfill them and enrich the planet."

You can see that embedded in this statement are all of the dimensional aspects: 5D—Conscious Vibration, 4D—Connect Humanity with the Divine, 3D—Fulfill them and Enrich the Planet. Each of you has an exalted purpose which can be found using this approach. The key is to look for the themes that repeat in the 7 Universal Life Purpose Elements and how they relate multidimensionally. Find flow from 5D Source/God/Goddess/All That Is into your dreams or inner calling in 4D that leads you into some exalted action in 3D.

Write down your answers from your life purpose elements/ your Life Purpose DNA™ here and notice what themes you have for each dimension and how they all relate to the other dimensions.

STEP 1—MY LIFE PURPOSE THEMES ARE:

5D:

_____

4D:

_____

3D:

_____

You'll see that you have a flow of energy that leads into the spiritual that finally manifests in form. You want to create a life purpose statement that reflects your purpose in life 3/4/5D and that all parts of yourself are being given expression. Try to start from the *being* level 5D, then filter it down through your *intuition* 4D, finally into the *practical expressions* in 3D. Let it come as a vision—let it "dream into you." It might take a couple of days or it might come to you as a flash of light. The important part is to see that ALL of you is reflected so that you can truly live on purpose. Make sure the common ideas like the Law of Attraction, your target market, etc., are clear and specific. What are you doing, for whom, and how in each of the different levels?

An example of this: a person chooses to focus on just one area or expression like being a watsu (water massage practitioner) who helps people get comfortable being embodied. This has all three multidimensional aspects in this one career:

5D: helping people feel their connectedness with the elements

4D: connecting to feeling a deeper level of what is going on inside of themselves

3D: helping them relax into just being in their bodies and experiencing their physicality

Here's an actual client who reframed a traditional career. Imagine being an attorney who connects with Source, listens to the angels, and then lets that guidance be how she advises with her adversarial clients for a harmonious result. You will have your own life purpose and many life purpose expressions. Your life purpose is the underlying reason why you do things and the expressions are the way at this point in time you are carrying it out.

Another possible case is a person who loves being with people and helping others. He becomes a boy scout, then eagle scout, and he tutors young people while he is still in high school. After high school, he pursues a teaching career to make money from his passion of helping people discover their own capabilities. But after a decade of teaching, he tires of the bureaucratic aspects of teaching and yearns for a new career. He finds a unique educational startup company who wants him to design curricula that reflect the young people's interests and aptitudes and best practices to help them learn subjects like math and science. In his fifties, he's tired of creating and wants to get back into the classroom, but doesn't want to teach in the traditional way, so he founds a charter school and becomes its administrator to make sure the school is run from a vision, not a bureaucracy.

Each of you will have many life purpose "expressions" like these examples, but you will only have ONE life purpose which is reflected in every activity throughout your life. It may appear different, but you can see that these people all had a desire to help people in some capacity to make the world a better place. When you write your statement, you will feel a sense of exaltation and peace—when it truly reflects who you are.

STEP 2—MY LIFE PURPOSE STATEMENT

Feel free to refine this as many times as you like and to have it be something you can craft over a period of time. Let it flow and let your multidimensional being have time to put energy into it and give you downloads of energy, insight and vision about your purpose as you craft and refine your life purpose statement. It can be long, short, an affirmation or whatever format really feels good to you.

My Life Purpose—Personal Mission Statement is:

_____

_____

_____

Once you feel satisfied with your life purpose statement, sit by yourself first and just take it in on all levels and own and honor yourself and your purpose. Then read it to friends and family that know you well. Ask them for their feedback and validation of how it truly expresses who they know you to be.

STEP 3—YOUR LIFE PURPOSE RETROSPECTIVE

Now, it's time to test out your life purpose statement and vision to see if it is accurate. It's time to do an honest Life Purpose Retrospective that means reviewing the major things you did during each five-year period of your life going back to childhood. Remember that your life purpose is always operating in your life as the Personal WHY for what you did. Your intention for everything on your list should be expressions of your life purpose that you feel are encompassed in your life purpose statement.

Even as a child, we had intentions for the actions that we took:

- 3D what did you want to accomplish and why?

- 4D you felt compelled to something without consciously knowing why, you were just led to be, do or have certain things—now ask yourself why was that important?

- 5D is all about the energy—where did you find yourself connected and embodied as something bigger than yourself?

This process of being is a way to use your life purpose to organize your life and career. The next part is owning your life purpose at all levels and seeing it expressed in how you live 3/4/5D. Feel yourself truly owning your life purpose and all of the ways that you have expressed it already in your life. Notice how you have or have not been expressing it—I say that you are either "being or becoming," so when you don't feel like you are living on purpose, you are preparing for what is to come—and how ultimately you can and will express your purpose. This step helps you truly own your experience and purpose.

STEP 4—CONNECTING WITH THE SOURCE & THE DIVINE

This step can be the most remarkable and influential for people because it takes everything that you have just learned about yourself, your purpose, and how you have already been manifesting it, and throws that up to Spirit for another look.

Imagine if you have fulfilled a particular life purpose expression, it might be time to move on and give your being the opportunity to communicate and convey to you what the best uses of your multidimensional energies might be. At this point in your life, it can just be a tweak to a vision or a major change in course that you have the opportunity to make. Often it sets you up for better ways to align with your life purpose from a place of creation and right livelihood.

Take time to do a meditation, create a vision board, ask in your dreams (or whatever methods you use) to connect with your higher power or Source. Some people prefer to be in nature and connect with something bigger than themselves. It could come in the form of a download, so be open to all the possibilities that present themselves for this information and guidance.

The guidance I received about what I am supposed to be, do or have that expresses my life purpose going forward is:

STEP 5—LIVING FROM YOUR PURPOSE
AND DIVINE CENTER

The final step is to LIVE IT—TO EMBODY YOUR PURPOSE IN ALL DIMENSIONS, to bring that energy through in all the things that you do. Each of us has an exalted reason for being here at this time and space. Now it is up to you to feel confident, courageous and express your purpose moment by moment in the world.

Remember that you want to feel and experience the expressions of your life purpose through all of your being (3/4/5D). The actions of 3D, the knowing and rightness of where you are (4D), and the infinite amounts of energy and excitement that you generate flowing through you (5D). Every person on the planet has this capacity and capability. It's time for you to step into yours now!

Deepak Chopra's book, *The Seven Spiritual Laws of Success*, describes the three criteria that you must have in what you do to achieve what I call your "High Havingness™" which means your inner fulfillment and outer success. They are:

1. You know you have a gift or talent in this lifetime.

2. You know how to use that talent in some type of service.

3. It must in some way benefit humanity and the planet.

Here are some examples of what this might look like in each of the Dimensions of Purpose that are expanded upon in my workbook, *111 Inspirational Life Purpose Quotes and Exercises to Find Your Purpose in Life*.

3D—Being a Lifestyle Entrepreneur

Some of the hallmarks of purpose for Lifestyle Entrepreneurs are people who:

- Want their lives geared around their purposes,
- Want the things they engage in to provide them personal meaning and fulfillment,
- Want fulfillment on their own terms and they are no longer driven by money and traditional success and values.

Lifestyle Entrepreneurs are very self-directed and they create their own paths and opportunities for themselves.

4D—Knowing You Are the Shift as a Visionary Change Agent

This involves a shift in consciousness and the ability to live from a place of flow and inner guidance. Some of the hallmarks of being a change agent at this level are to know:

- That we are connected to the divine in some way,
- That we align our lives and actions from a place of guidance using our free will to manifest that vision,
- That we seek the divine spark of light in all life.

This is where people feel strongly connected with their intuition and the unseen realms for direction and confirmation about their paths.

5D—Being a Beacon of Light as Resonance for the New Age

This level of being encompasses being a light worker in the many different approaches from Reiki, to light body work, or to deep meditation where you become a frequency that you resonate and embody in this dimension. People working in a 5D purpose express:

- A harmony and resonance that they hold for the benefit of the planet.
- They embody the higher dimensional frequencies and also the frequencies of the dreamtime.
- Their lives are focused on *being*, not *doing*.

Each of us is geared for success and fulfillment on all levels as long as we are meeting these three simple criteria that express our purposes. Start living your life from this conscious multidimensional place today!

THE BODY-MIND CONNECTION

Lynn Waldrop

"To keep the body in good health is a duty . . . otherwise we
shall not be able to keep our mind strong and clear."

—Buddha

There are so many modalities around today, and some of them
tell you to get rid of the mind while others absolutely revere
it—what if neither was a truth? If the point is for us to be in
oneness, with no separation, then why would we separate our
mind from our beings, our bodies or anything else? And on the
other hand, why would the mind be the one thing that rules
us? For me life is literally finding a way of NO separation to
anything—my mind, other people, or my body or even all the
bodies that comprise us. (So many like to separate them into
the etheric, ketheric, metetheric, astral, spiritual, emotional—
what if even that was a way to separate us from ourselves?)

So this chapter is on the Mind/Body Connection—if we
didn't separate them, but instead employed them to work for
us and with us, what could we create? And how much fun

could life and creation be then? My motto is, "Life is Play-Doh. If you don't like what you have created—laugh at it, squish it, and create something new!"

The Mind

My whole life I was considered smart, especially since I possessed both kinds of "smart" according to my parents. They said it was a rarity to possess both "book-smart" and "common-sense smart." But truthfully, where did that get me? I would speak my mind and get in lots of trouble with adults, and I was always a *smarty-pants,* which got me in trouble with other kids. It was really a double-edged sword. I was always who my parents turned to when putting electronics together like dishwashers, scanners, and other devices, even at a young age. At the age of nine my family got our first dishwasher, and I was in charge of assembly when my father couldn't make it work. I skipped a step as well, and when we did a test run, soap came pouring out of every seal of the dishwasher, filling the entire kitchen—and I was punished. Why did they put all that faith in a nine-year-old? Darn that mind!

I was also called "strong-willed" a lot, but don't people really mean "strong-minded" when they say that? These terms really mean you know what you want, and you have the gall to ask for it, create it or be it. We are taught to "ask and ye shall receive," but you really aren't supposed to have the gall to ask because that will make you self-centered! This reality is SO confusing!

People use the mind for a lot of things, but one particular use is to *judge everything* around them. My parents judged me as being "smarter" than they (even at the age of nine). Who do you deem smarter, more important, richer, poorer, better, more confident than you? What if instead of using the mind as a comparison machine, we learned to harness that power and used it to create what we REALLY desire in life?

As I got older I would sit down and talk to a stranger here and there, and my grandma would say, "Lynny, you realize no one else can see him?" I had no idea he had passed away. I thought it was normal, and everyone saw him sitting there. But she cultivated those intuitive powers in me. (She read her astrology every day in the newspaper!) Then I took a psychic awareness class from one of my life mentors, Joyce Rennolds. She immediately had us do readings on each other. I was thinking, "I don't know how to do this."

She said, "Just hold her hands, calm your mind, and say whatever comes up." I will never forget that evening, it was as if it was yesterday, and it was the first day of my life.

So where does the mind end and intuition or awareness begin? When does it become greater than us? I never liked "collective consciousness" because it still felt like something had control of me, like a queen bee, the Matrix, or something. I am a Pioneer of New Frontiers, I AM the Queen Bee and as a part of the ALL, the EVERYTHING—why can't the consciousness of everything work together for each of us? To me that is the spark I strive for every day—the knowing of which molecules to play with and to be those molecules for everything else as well.

The Body

Oh the body, oh how I have abused thee, let me count the ways! Some modalities/religions don't come right out and say "Dying is the greatest thing ever because you get to get out of this skin suit and be free to fly around and go anywhere you want," but that's insinuated. Others make the whole life experience about the body. Again, what if neither was a truth? What if we could harness the energy the body provides, the consciousness of the body, and employ it to work with all of the other working, living parts to create something magnificent?

I used to fly above my bed with "angels" when I was a small child, until I heard my mom walking down the hallway and I fell to the bed. When I was scolded for jumping on the bed, my mind said, "Tell the truth and you will be rewarded," but sadly that was not the case. I told the truth and was spanked for lying because it wasn't possible for me to fly above my bed, let alone talk with angels. I never flew again. My mind bought my mom's point of view and locked it in every cell. How many ideas or concepts have we all locked into our bodies that weren't even our ideas in the first place?

I developed so early as a child that by the time I was nine-and-a-half-years old, I was 5'4" tall, with a C-cup bra size and a size nine shoe. Being a psychic child (as we all are) I heard everyone's mind commenting on how I looked, why it was good or bad, and what they would like to do to that body and more. So what is the mind's first defense?—JUDGE IT—which I was very successful in doing! But my body had a mind of its own and body parts liked to escape from my clothing on a regular basis—swim suits, dresses and more! The response was not good. In this reality breasts and other body parts are to remain covered at all times and, therefore, my body and I went to war! How dare the body get me in trouble, too! So Lynn the Being, Lynn's mind and Lynn's body waged a long war against each other. (Any of this sounding familiar to you—the war part, I mean?)

We would never tell our children to judge their bodies, so why do we do it to ourselves? Where is the kindness in all that? Do you realize how much *dis*-ease I find in people's bodies that are a result of the absolute judgment and unkindness they have heaped upon it?

You chose to come here, be on this planet, live this life, and occupy this body—do you want to stay at war with your best friends while you are here? Or would you rather create your life as one amazing play-date with your best pals ever—your mind and your body?

The Body-Mind Connection

What if your mind was like a muscle? It needs to be exercised, cultivated, and challenged! When the mind is a weak muscle, then the self-doubt, self-loathing, depression, sadness, and endless mind-chatter moves in like a parasite and takes over. I don't know about you but my mind gets bored! So I send it out on jobs—go find new clients, go find a really cool place to vacation next. Give it something constructive to do for you! That is employing the molecules!

Your entire being is acoustical, and that is one of the reasons I have practiced vibrational therapies for over twenty years (sound, color, light and consciousness). Everything is energy including us; we are all just hanging around vibrating at different rates. What would it take for you to open your mind, stretch it even, to new possibilities about what you are truly capable of? I love the series *Through the Wormhole* with Morgan Freeman. Their shows on consciousness and what science is trying to prove is fascinating! They can now demonstrate that you can be in one room and I in a different sound-proof room blind-folded, show you photos of emotional events, and we both will emit the emotion at the same time! They are proving that our thoughts fly across space. Okay, we already knew that and science is just catching up, but how do we utilize this in our daily life? Consciously use it!

So I hear you saying, "Okay, but how do we consciously use acoustics?" We have been taught to live so much of our lives on auto-pilot that not many people walk around consciously doing or choosing anything. Let's start there.

1. Have fun with it—Life is Play-Doh.

2. Detox the TFEs from the mind and body (TFE=thoughts, feelings & emotions).

3. Exercise the mind muscle.

4. Fall in love with your body and listen to it!

5. Learn to communicate with everything.

6. Be the largest employer in the universe!

#1—HAVE FUN WITH IT

Who decided that life had to be taken SO seriously? Do you see trees worried about how many leaves they grew this year, and what other trees might think or say about that? Do you see a river worried that his friend the rock will be upset if he chooses a new route? Why do we worry about such trivial nonsense? Do we have to ask the Universe, God, Allah, Source, that consciousness that permeates all things, "Do I deserve to take a breath now, am I worthy yet, please?" before each breath? The answer is NO. Yet I see lot of people sitting around waiting for something to drop into their laps. We are creative beings; we create all the time; and if we aren't creating what we would really like, uh-oh, yeah, we are creating that stuff that we really didn't want.

So life is your playground. Get every molecule of your being, your mind and your body involved in your life! That is conscious living and conscious creating!

#2—DETOX THE TFES FROM THE MIND AND BODY

Yes, we are acoustical beings; however, have you ever noticed that some energies feel more dense than others? When a thought, feeling or emotion (TFEs I call them) has a charge—meaning it still affects you in some way—that data is stored in your cells. It becomes your programming, and you default to that programming without even knowing why most of the time. And then the mind gets the bad rap because people say, "It's that mind chatter causing the problem." What if it has gone past that, and literally the body is storing that information in little databases? We need to detox the mind and body and get rid of all that programming so we can consciously choose what we desire to create! Remember the old adage, "It's not what goes in your mouth that makes you sick, but what comes out of your mouth."

All TFEs create your world. What if we just chose unbridled joy for a day—how might our life and world change? And I don't mean this from that, "Oh, look at all the fake, woo-woo, pseudo-happy people that have no problems." I mean in our real lives. Acknowledge—yes, I just created a pile of crap. Now I can sit in my steaming pile of crap OR hmmm, I can say, "Life is Play-Doh." I'm going to squish this pile and create something new! Jacob Liberman said so profoundly that it is when we take something that was meant to be fluid and try to make it solid that causes dis-ease! These TFEs create solidity in our worlds and the body!

Here is a list of some TFEs from the mind and body that I have found to be the most destructive on the body and life:

Grief	Judgment	Unworthy/ Undeserving
Anger	Abandonment	Obligation
Victim	Shock/Terror	Taking everything personally
Unkindness	Trauma/Drama	Jealousy/ Suspicion
Guilt	Fear	Sadness/ Depression
Sacrifice	Abuse	Need to Control everything
Shame	Holding onto Hurts	Doubt (especially of YOU!)

We have the capacity to be every energy, so I am not judging these energies as *bad*. But what I am saying is that if you judge them as a bad or negative emotion, and then hold onto it, you re-program your cells! Then it becomes a pattern that you then function from, and this is how people get to "push your buttons." What if you had a moment of grief, and you allowed yourself to move through it; and when it no longer served you or you got bored with it, you said, "Okay, time to pick something else"? I know this might sound like a strange way to live life, but it is so freeing. And in truth, it isn't so strange after all. When you were a child, you played with one toy and then two seconds later put it down and got another, and kept on switching toys. We, the beings that we are, are so dynamic and ever-changing that we can give ourselves the freedom to do just that—change! Change your mind, change the plan, change how you feel. Just because most of the world would get angry if someone did "A" (whatever that act is), does that mean you have to choose to get angry? Why can't you be the child and choose something different? Do you have to follow the programming society has, or can you make up your own mind?

And what is this idea that we only use 10 percent of our brain? —like the idea that Jean brought up earlier, that we only use a portion of our DNA and the rest is *junk* DNA. Our mind is a mystery; there is SO much more to it than scientists really know. Information is everywhere today, and I see so many people actually LIMITING themselves due to the information rather than using it as a springboard to catapult them into something greater. When you hear that someone can do something amazing, do you think, "I don't believe that," or, "I wish I could do that"? Or do you ask, "Wow, that's possible? How do I create that and more in my life?" What if that intuition or awareness actually utilizes the other 90 percent? What if by *detoxing* the mind and body we can get rid of the programming in the cells that actually limits us? We have lived many lives and come to a lot of conclusions over those lifetimes. So what drives us to do what we do in this lifetime? Conscious living or cellular programming? For most of my life I couldn't wear turtleneck sweaters, choker necklaces or anything somewhat tight around my neck. After years of past-life regressions I was aware that I had been strangled to death several times. I had no conscious awareness of that, yet in this lifetime I was driven to despise anything close to my neck. Once I released that from my cells, I could wear a turtleneck sweater with no problems. And I don't even believe that we have to look at this programming one situation at a time. I believe our bodies and mind are SO brilliant that we can just send a frequency through our bodies to release the programming, like pushing the re-set button, and allow the cell to go back to the factory default—total health and wellness! Detox that mind and body!

#3 EXERCISE THE MIND MUSCLE

In metaphysics I always heard a lot about "mind chatter," where self-talk (usually negative) would creep into almost any situation—like you are an out-of-control train and the "mind chatter" is the engineer driving it off the tracks. So who is really in control here—you or your mind? Have you ever been "out of your mind"?

I am not really a fan of affirmations or positive self-talk. Most people I see use this to repeat a statement in rote that they don't really believe they can have in the first place. It's kind of a way to trick the Universe into giving it to them anyway. Let's get something straight here—YOU are the Creator of your world, the Picasso of this grand, live painting you call life! Waiting for the Universe (or anything else) to bless you with something is not how it works. Look deep inside. What do you really desire to create?

- Money or abundance
- Health

- More joy
- New job
- Peace and kindness
- Relationships

Whatever it is, we have to change this mind-set of how this mind muscle works!

1. Stop the mind chatter now. I created mp3s that detox the body as well as the mind. One called the "Mind Detox" is most beneficial for deleting the programming of grief, depression and other TFEs mentioned on the previous pages. The programming is where we made a decision at some point, or were implanted with others' points of view, and now that programming runs at even a cellular level in a loop. Have you ever known someone caught in a gripping loop of fear or sadness? Why not use frequencies to transform energy? There are many ways—find what works for you.

2. KNOW to the core of your Being that you can truly create or be anything. (If you can't believe in you, know that I do!)

3. Don't let anyone or anything stop you from what you truly desire to create.

4. Be willing to do the work to get all the energies moving.

5. Ask every molecule to jump in and play with you to create this.

6. Let the molecules do their job (meaning don't be a control freak and try to choke it to death)!

I see so many folks who don't get what they asked for say, "Well, I guess it wasn't meant to be," or, "All things in divine time (and I guess it's not my divine time)." What if it all has to do with the energy of SURRENDER? We have been taught to surrender—to yield to the power of another—which doesn't fit into creation. In oneness every molecule is working to create; no one molecule is greater than another.

#4 FALL IN LOVE WITH YOUR BODY (AND LISTEN TO IT)!

I used to be one of those people who was never inside their body. It was so much more fun to astral/dimensionally travel, that why the heck would I want to just stay here? I would never really admit that I hated my body out loud, but it was always right there. My weight was always up 50 pounds or down 50 pounds every five years of my adult life, and in between I was either on the uphill climb or downhill slide. I was the queen of DIEting! Note the spelling. I even began doing Triathlons in an attempt to create a lifestyle change where I wouldn't have to DIEt anymore. But when you are exercising six hours a day, and you are a size 4 for the first time in your life since the fourth grade, and your teammates call you "the big girl," that's just darn frustrating. Triathlons didn't work for me anymore. I then moved to the State of Depression and tried every anti-depressant on the planet. It wasn't until I really just decided one day that this had to change, and I wasn't feeling that way anymore, that a change of heart and a change of mind occurred, and I was able to climb my way out of the depths. A part of that was learning to LOVE the Skin You're In! Here are some helpful tips:

1. When you get out of the shower and you are completely naked, look in a full-length mirror. What do you see? What

do you hear? If you hear that "ugh, look at that sagging and look at that cellulite . . ." then

- Have gratitude for your body. Do you have two feet and two legs that allow you to stand and walk? Do you have two arms and two hands that allow you to touch and do things? Do you have eyes that allow you to see this beautiful world and ears to hear the birds sing? Then you have things about your body to be grateful for, even if you have to start there.

2. Again, naked in the full-length mirror, pull up what you look like in your partner or lover's eyes. I'll bet you look different! Usually they are less critical of our bodies than we are. Cherish that, be that.

3. Even if you aren't a car person (I wasn't), if money were no object, what would be the sexiest car you could think of? Don't go any further until you choose! Use all of your senses—what are the colors, what does it feel like, smell like, how do you feel in the car?

- Now embody that feeling for you—you ARE that sexy vehicle! How would your world change if you walked down the street BEing that sexy beast?

4. Look around at people of all sizes, shapes and colors. What do you see? Their imperfections or their attributes? Learn to admire both women's and men's bodies. My whole life, I never could admire a woman's body because I so judged my own body!

5. And every time you go back to judging your body, go back to Step 2 and detox the TFEs in the mind and body!

I talk to my body all the time—I ask it what it wants to eat, where it wants to drink, what would be fun in terms of movement (we hate exercise) for the day, would it like to play in the sun or rain . . . just about anything. The body has its own consciousness or intelligence, so how can we tap into that to assist in the creation of a greater life for ourselves?

#5 LEARN TO COMMUNICATE WITH EVERYTHING

Every day I wake up and ask for all the cells of my body to pull in the energy, vibration and frequency of anything they require for perfect health for me. Everything is energy! (Have I mentioned this before?) Energy cannot be killed, only transformed. So how can we transform all of the energies of lack, powerlessness, sadness and so forth into Joy, Abundance, and Magnificence? What if you just asked?

I go outside and talk with all of the plants in my yard and garden. I talk with rocks, and they tell me stories of where they have been and come from. I talk with entities, and not just dead humans. I talk to the oceans and the animals in it. I talk with the clouds and weather and the earth, and I even talk with the smallest of molecules. I use the work "talk" loosely, as it is more of a telepathy in the return conversation.

But for those of you who doubt, or believe I am delusional, remember one of my gifts in this lifetime is The Body Channel. I energetically dive into bodies, and the bodies "tell" or "show" me where dis-ease or problem areas are. And many times these bodies show me things that aren't logical or that I can't possibly know. I can tell you that organs are missing from surgical procedures, I can tell a woman what part of her cycle she is in, I can tell you which vertebrae are out, and I have even had organs sing me certain songs. When I tell the body's owner the song choice, they flip because that is a song they sing or hum all the time (and I am not talking usual songs, but ones more like "O Sole Mio" or "Heard it Through the Grapevine"). So for me the goal is the capacity to communicate with everything—isn't that the oneness we all talk about?

Everyone has the capacity to communicate with every molecule in the universe.

1. It just takes a little practice and play time.

2. Have no expectations of how you will receive the information.

3. Ask lots of questions; never stop asking.

4. You cannot doubt the info you receive.

5. You have to ask to receive more information each time, please!

6. And a little gratitude for yourself and your talents never hurts!

Many people block their receiving of the information because they expect it to come a certain way. It isn't really blocking because you are receiving it, but you don't know how to translate the data. For instance, earthquake activity I usually feel in my lower back, and water activity like hurricanes I usually feel in my stomach; entities can feel like pressure or make you out of breath. Are these the way you would expect to sense them?

I see many healers working on people and they simply do "the process," whatever that is for that modality. Not me!

Every little thing I perceive I ask their body, "Oh, what's that?" This is like the ultimate playground for me! And I just kept asking questions and asking to receive more information each time, until I built up that muscle.

#6 EMPLOY THE UNIVERSE

Now that you have . . .

- Cleared out the TFEs that limit You the BEing, You the mind and You the body so you can begin to work together as one Infinite BEing,
- Learned to exercise the mind muscle,
- Fallen in love with your body,
- Learned to communicate with every molecule,

. . . how do you employ the Universe?

Simple—invite every molecule in the universe to come and play.

Gosh, that's too simple, Lynn! But is it really true?

The problem is that most of us would rather do everything ourselves! We might complain that no one joins in to help (even when we ask), but really most of us would just rather do it ourselves. Why? Others disappoint, they don't get it right, we are faster . . . we can make excuses all day long. Just because you CAN do everything, does that mean you should always choose that?

I learned a long time ago as a single mom that I spent my weekends cleaning house and cutting the yard, and there was no time left for me or my son. For $35, I could have someone cut my grass, and for $75, someone could clean the house. I then looked at what I was making per hour and learned it was cheaper to pay someone else!

Why not employ every molecule to bring more money, relationships, travel, sex, or whatever it is that you desire? This isn't greedy or selfish! If a child makes you a mud pie, especially for you as a gift, do you push it away and say, no thanks? You receive it as the gift it is; it doesn't matter that it is a mud pie because the child made that mud pie just for you! The molecules are like you—always creating—and they are just waiting for you or anyone to ask! There is a certain TV/Internet company (who will remain nameless) that doesn't have the best customer service, and it takes forever to get them to fix any problems with the bill. I don't have time to sit around while they pass me around from department to department. So I ask the molecules to tell me exactly when the person who will know the answer (and be able to fix it within five to ten minutes) is on duty and ready for me. And BAM! As soon as I get the awareness of that little timer going off, I call, and sure enough, I am down within ten minutes!

What if being the largest employer of the Universe actually made your life a little easier? Could you handle that?

In the beginning I asked—If the point is for us to be in oneness, with no separation, then why would we separate our mind from our BEings, our bodies or anything else? If we didn't separate from anything but instead employed everything to work *for* us and *with* us, what could we create? And how much fun could life and creation be then?

"Life is Play-Doh. If you don't like what you have created—laugh at it, squish it, and create something new!"

WRAPPING IT UP

Life is a grand adventure, filled with choices and opportunities. It's our desire that you have gleaned a few nuggets from this book that will help you to make those choices to be of the highest vibration possible.

Here is my challenge for you: where will you go from here? If you could have ANYTHING manifest for you within the next five minutes, what would you create—right here, right now? Breathe into your heart center, and open the door to the field of potential and allow that to flow to you and be grateful for this gift.

We are in a huge period of evolution now. We are being given the opportunity to let go of everything that has no value for us anymore, and when we create the space for something new, we will attract things that have real intrinsic value—at the core level, rather than value based on outer ideas and ideals.

The fulfillment of all your desires is possible now. GO for it!

Deep love,

Jean Adrienne

ABOUT THE AUTHORS

JEAN ADRIENNE is an author, radio show host, world traveler, financially independent entrepreneur, and developer of the InnerSpeak™ Breakthrough Coaching and Therapy Process. Her passion is creating quantum change in her own life and sharing it with others through in-person or Skype coaching/ clearing sessions. Jean has a BA in Psychology from Florida State University and has completed the four-year Education for Ministry from The University of the South. Jean's books—*Soul Adventures, Reframe Your World: Conscious Creation in the New Reality*, and her latest, *Power Tools: The Ultimate Owner's Manual for Personal Empowerment*; and her amazing decks of empowerment cards—*The InnerSpeak™ Cards* and *Reconnecting Soul: 142 DNA Activation Cards*—are all available on *Amazon.com* and *http://www.jeanadrienne.com/Store*

LESLIE AMERSON is an author, teacher, speaker, tele-summit host, spiritual intuitive, and a Life, Business Entrepreneur, and Nutrition Coach. Her passion is empowering others to generate the change they are seeking in their lives, relationships, body, business, or career. Life is supposed to be

FUN . . . understanding emotions and learning how to forgive will get you to the FUN parts more often. Leslie teaches workshops, intensives, and does one-on-one sessions with her clients. She has a BA in Business Management from the University of Phoenix, is a Coaches Alliance Certified Business Entrepreneur Coach and an Institute of Integrative Nutrition Certified Nutrition Coach. Leslie's book, *The Adventures of Jordyn Lane ~ The Disappearing Child,* penned under L.J. Jackson, is available on *Amazon.com.* Her website is: *www.leslieamerson.com*

JULIA GRIFFIN is a tele-summit host, intuitive healer, and writer. She has successfully healed and transformed the lives of thousands of clients for the past eight years by helping her clients discover how to discern the inner voice of their own intuitive wisdom or the True Self. Julia sees and reads energy to find its resonance with the soul and gently guides clients through this amazing process that she learned from wolves and nature. She helps others resolve the challenges of life, ranging from business enterprises to highly personal issues. Her website is: *www.onetruself.com*

LAURIE HUSTON is a Professional Intuitive Counselor. Her passion is developing clearing and healing techniques to assist her clients. Laurie incorporates her professional qualifications that include a bachelor's degree in Social Work and Neuro-Linguistic Programming (NLP), amongst others, with her intuitive counseling and natural clairsentient and claircognizant abilities.

Laurie has been on her spiritual path for the past twenty years, and during that time acquired through extensive studies, teachings, and sacred texts, over twenty-five different healing modalities that she regularly uses. Her website is: *www.intuitivesoul.com*

KATHLEEN O'KEEFE-KANAVOS is an author, inspirational speaker, mentor, and world traveler. She was born to a military family, raised in Europe, graduated from Munich International High School in Germany, has a degree in Special Education from Keene Teachers College, taught Special Education for ten years and Psychology at the University of South Florida. Kathleen is a two-time breast cancer survivor and has penned her first book, *Surviving Cancerland: The Intuitive Aspects of Healing.* Kathleen is an active participant with the R. A. Bloch Cancer Foundation and WE-CAN self-help organization, contributing writer for *Cape Women Online Magazine*, Twitter's *C4Women,* Colette Baron-Reid's *Intuition Now,* Examiner.com, *Writer's Digest Community, Scribblerati*, and numerous blogs. Coming soon is Kathleen's second book, *Surviving Recurrence in Cancerland: The Dream World and Healing.* Her website is: *www.survivingcancerland.com*

LINDA MINNICK works with individuals and organizations, helping them build their dreams, accelerate their results, and create richer, more fulfilling lives. Linda is a specialist in transformational thinking and has shared the stage with world-renowned teachers such as Mary Morrissey, Bob Proctor, and Michael Beckwith. As a sought-after coach, speaker, and trainer, Linda teaches transformational coaching and workshops to individuals and organizations around the country. Linda helps her clients ignite the potential within them to attain the results they have been looking for and gives them the tools to continue on that upward spiral of fulfillment and success. Linda is a Certified Life Coach, Professional PSYCH-K® Facilitator, Certified Sales Coach, Certified Doreen Virtue Card Reader, speaker, author, and entrepreneur. Her website is: *www.lindaminnick.com*

Using the principles and practices of the Genie System for the past twenty years, MAUREEN ST. GERMAIN has created a life filled with love, success, and happiness. In her latest book, *Be A Genie*, the author and intuitive assists people in meeting, and surpassing, their life dreams and goals using the laws of quantum physics and sacred geometry. She has traveled and taught workshops worldwide for almost twenty years. Author of the Amazon.com bestseller, *Beyond the Flower of Life*, Maureen has been teaching the MerKaBa Meditation and Higher Self connection to audiences worldwide since 1994. Her website is: *www.maureenstgermain.com*

SUZANNE STRISOWER is an author, radio show host, blogger, motivational speaker, life and career coach, intuitive, and healer on a mission to get more people to not just live life, but to prosper and thrive! Coming from a place of positive thinking and optimism, Suzanne advocates Lifestyle Prepping in her works. She is the author of three books including her nationally acclaimed awards-winning *111 Inspirational Life Purpose Quotes and Exercises to Find Your Purpose in Life* and *The Runes of the Four Realms.* Suzanne has chapters in many other books including chapters for the best-selling *Wake Up Women* book series. She is the founder of Living Well Talk Radio Network and currently hosts three shows: *Living Life on Purpose, The Doctor's INN,* and *Your Life and Purpose Revealed.* Her website is: *www. susannestrisower.com*

LYNN WALDROP is certified in Color Therapy, Tuning Fork Therapy, Reiki, and Access Consciousness. As a medical intuitive, she is known as "The Body Channel," and energetically dives into each of the thirteen body systems of her clients. The body talks to her, showing her "problem areas" and the means to change them while she is in there! Lynn empowers her clients to create and generate change in their own life and body—life is to enjoy, not be destroyed! Lynn is also an accredited CE Provider for Massage Therapists and Hypnotherapists in the U.S. Her website is *www.LynnWaldrop.com*

RELATED TITLES

If you enjoyed *Realities of Creation*, you may also enjoy other Rainbow Ridge titles. Read more about them at *www.rainbowridgebooks.com*.

God's Message to the World: You've Got Me All Wrong
by Neale Donald Walsch

The Secret of Effortless Being
by Ronny Hatchwell and Zach Sivan

Rita's World
by Frank DeMarco

Soul Courage
by Tara-jenelle Walsch

Quantum Economics
by Amit Goswami

Coming Full Circle: Ancient Teachings for a Modern World
by Lynn Andrews

Consciousness: Bridging the Gap Between Conventional Science and the New Super Science of Quantum Mechanics
by Eva Herr

Messiah's Handbook: Reminders for the Advanced Soul
by Richard Bach

Blue Sky, White Clouds
by Eliezer Sobel

Inner Vegas: Creating Miracles, Abundance, and Health
by Joe Gallenberger

Your Soul Remembers: Accessing Your Past Lives through Soul Writing
by Joanne DiMaggio

When the Horses Whisper: The Wisdom of Wise and Sentient Beings
by Rosalyn W. Berne, Ph.D.

Lessons in Courage
by Bonnie Glass-Coffin and don Oscar Miro-Quesada

The Healing Curve
by Sara Chetkin

God Within
by Patti Conklin

Conversations with God for Parents
by Neale Donald Walsch, Laurie Farley, and Emily Filmore

Dance of the Electric Hummingbird
by Patricia Walker

Rainbow Ridge Books publishes spiritual, metaphysical, and self-help titles, and is distributed by Square One Publishers in Garden City Park, New York.

To contact authors and editors, peruse our titles, and see submission guidelines, please visit our website at *www.rainbowridgebooks.com.*